The P.E.I. Multicultural Council Cookbook

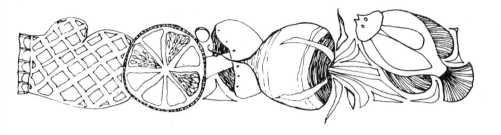

MANY CULTURES
MANY COOKS

Ragweed Press

&

P.E.I. Multicultural Council

1987

ISBN 0-920304-76-1

Ragweed Press
P.O. Box 2023
Charlottetown, Prince Edward Island
Canada C1A 7N7

Editors: Lesley Brothers, Heather Irving
Illustrations: Judy Whitaker
Project Co-ordinator: Heather Irving
Book Design: Cape Bear Associates
Typesetting: Braemar Publishing Limited

With thanks to the Department of Communications for its kind support.

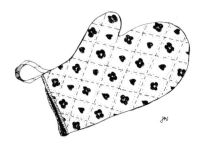

Canadian Cataloguing in Publication Data
Main entry under title:
Many cultures, many cooks
Includes index.
ISBN 0-920304-76-1
1. Cookery, International. 2. Cookery—Prince Edward Island. I.
Prince Edward Island Multicultural Council.
TX725.A1M36   1987   641.59   C87-094396-0

MANY CULTURES
MANY COOKS

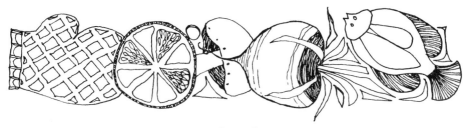

Acknowledgements

Many thanks to the following volunteers who contributed their time, recipes and advice.

Nawal Abdala
Etta Anderson
Barb Arsenault
Josephine Arsenault
Ev Beagan
Irene Bujara
Monica Choo
Florence Cunningham
Patricia Déaz-Reddin
Sr. Gemma Dunn
Maria-Elizabeth Fricke
Eva Fuhrmeister
Hilde Gerharz
Sharda Gupta
Maria Hager
Eleanor Kremer
Leti LaRosa
Anca Laxer
Lorraine Levi
Joan MacFarlane
Anne MacKinnon
Myrtle MacLeod

Tilly MacLeod
Jacob Mal
Kati Mason
Hedy Ochsner
Asifa Rahman
Jean Rashed
Estelle Reddin
Doreen Sark
Ray Sark
Sr. Rebecca Sark
Rob Roy Pipe Band
    and Highland Dancers
    Cookbook—Kingston, Ont.
Ann Sherman
Rosalie Simeone
Nadine Smith
George Steiger
Lila Tweel
Annie Valkenburg
Dianne Vanderaa
Katie Van Ekris
Laura Zakem

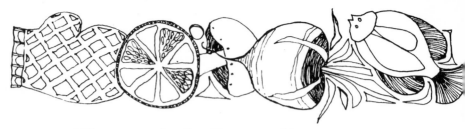

Financial Contributors

Allison's Hair Design
Birt's Transmission Sales
Canton Cafe
Harold Keller Insurance Associates Ltd.
Hutcheson's Fashion Plus
Island Furriers Ltd.
Jean's Cake Decorating and Supplies
Linda's Coffee Shop
Pinocchio's Children's Wear
Realty One Real Estate
Rogers Hardware
Root Cellar Health Foods
Sea Treat Restaurant
Town and Country Restaurant
Tweel's Gift Shop
Zakem's Real Estate

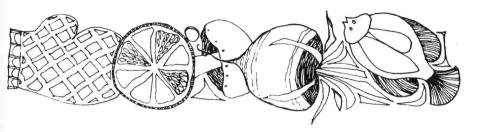

Contents

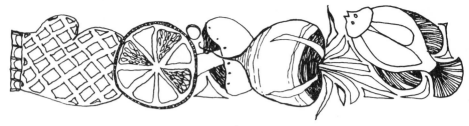

Introduction

People from over seventy-five different countries live on Prince Edward Island. Although these countries represent diverse traditions and beliefs, one thing they share is the importance of food in their cultures. Food helps to define a culture and to reveal its details and subtleties. This cookbook will introduce you to the foods of many different countries. We hope it will broaden your understanding and appreciation of the cultural diversity that is at your doorstep.

Over the years, Prince Edward Island has been blessed with some of the best cooks found anywhere. These cooks represent the finest cooking traditions from around the world. In 1983 the Multicultural Council put out a call for recipes. Within a year the Council had over a thousand submissions. The cookbook project was seen as a way to heighten awareness about multiculturalism, and to raise money for the important work of the Council.

The present cookbook committee started its work in March of 1986. Previous volunteer committees collected and typed the recipes. Our thanks go to all the contributors and volunteers who helped with this work.

We inherited a huge box full of the most interesting recipes imaginable. Our first task was to go through all the recipes and choose the ones we would use in the book. Unfortunately, there was simply no way we could produce a 500-page tome of multicultural delicacies.

The committee met Thursday mornings for a year. It was a labour of love. We met around the big table in the board room at the Multicultural Centre, and used it as we would a kitchen table, to read recipes and to make decisions. We shared our cultures, foods, customs and traditions, and talked about everything from our children and families, to food additives, diets and global peace.

It wasn't easy choosing recipes. Often a recipe was rejected for what any self-respecting cook would call the flimsiest of reasons—because it was a duplicate, because we had enough from that category, because we had too many from this country and not enough from that country, because we needed more desserts . . . and on and on. There were so many things to consider. What we wanted in the end was a well-balanced cookbook, consisting of representative and unique recipes. We wanted recipes from each of the ethnocultural groups that belonged to the Council, plus samples from other countries as well. We tried our best to meet this objective. If your favourite recipe is missing, or if your favourite cuisine isn't represented, please accept our regrets.

Somehow we did it. We managed to choose nearly two hundred recipes and to decide on a format and production plan. When the Council's board of directors agreed with our recommendation to let Ragweed Press publish the cookbook, we knew we had a winner. Ragweed's interest in the book was very significant. The whole project fell into place when Libby Oughton and Laurie Brinklow offered to get involved. They believed in the project from the start and did their best to turn a possibility into a reality. It was fitting that the Island's only publishing company, a woman's company, took on the project and brought it to fruition. Food is an important part of women's culture, and from the beginning the cookbook was the almost exclusive domain of women. Our thanks go to Libby and Laurie, and again to all the multicultural women who helped with the project.

And now a word about our cookbook. Be daring! Be experimental! Be inventive! Be flexible, and be prepared for a few surprises! Multicultural cooking, if we can coin a phrase, means all these things. If the recipe doesn't look the way you think it should, if there's too much of one spice or not enough of another to suit your taste, adjust. Each of the recipes came from someone's kitchen. As editors, we decided not to worry about consistency in weights and measures. We accepted and kept the recipes as they were received, re-wording only when necessary for the sake of clarity. All ingredients are available on the Island, either at supermarkets, natural food stores or specialty stores. We hope that you enjoy the spirit and the challenge of multicultural cooking.

Bon Appetit!

COOKBOOK COMMITTEE:
Lesley Brothers, Maria Hager, Heather Irving, Jean Rashed, Dianne Vanderaa.

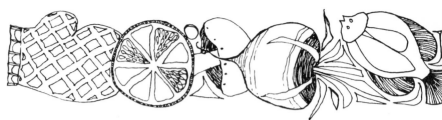

Approximate Metric Conversions

Imperial Measurements	Approximate Metric Conversion
⅛ tsp	0.5 mL
¼ tsp	1 mL
½ tsp	2 mL
1 tsp	5 mL
1 tbsp	15 mL
1 coffee measure	25 mL
2 tbsp (1 oz)	30 mL
¼ cup	50 mL
⅓ cup	80 mL
½ cup	125 mL
⅔ cup	160 mL
¾ cup	180 mL
1 cup	250 mL
1 pint	625 mL
1 quart	1000 mL or 1.25 litre
¼ pound	125 g
½ pound	250 g
¾ pound	350 g
1 pound	500 g

Converting to Metric

To change	to	Multiply by
teaspoons	mL	5
tablespoons	mL	15
ounces	mL	28
cups	litres	0.24

Acadia

One-Hour Rolls

1 envelope active dry yeast
1 cup boiling water
5 tbsp margarine
1 tbsp white sugar
1 tbsp salt
1 cup milk
1 egg
5 cups flour

Follow directions for dissolving the yeast as on the envelope. Combine boiling water, margarine, sugar and salt. Stir to melt margarine. Add milk and cool until lukewarm. Add beaten egg and yeast. Work in flour. Place dough in a greased bowl. (For faster rising, place the bowl in the kitchen sink with hot water.) Cover the dough with a damp cloth and let rise for 15 minutes. Punch down and let rise for 15 minutes more. Divide into pieces and shape into round rolls. Place on a greased baking sheet. Cover and let rise until doubled in bulk. Brush lightly with cold water to improve crustiness. Bake at 350°F for 15 to 20 minutes.

Corn Bread

¼ cup shortening
¼ cup sugar
1 egg
1 cup milk (or buttermilk)
1 cup cornmeal
1 cup flour
2 tsp baking powder, or
  1 tsp baking soda, if using buttermilk

Cream shortening. Stir in sugar and egg. Combine cornmeal, flour and baking powder or soda. Add to shortening mixture alternately with milk, stirring just enough to moisten. Pour into greased loaf pan. Bake at 375°F for 30 to 40 minutes or until done.

Potato Pancakes

3 cups grated potato
1 onion, finely chopped
1 egg, beaten slightly
¼ cup flour
½ tsp baking powder
¼ cup hot water
salt and pepper
vegetable oil or pork fat

Drain surplus liquid from grated potato. Add chopped onion, egg and flour. Mix well. Add baking powder to hot water, pour over flour mixture and mix well. Add salt and pepper to taste. Heat oil or fat in frying pan. Brown pancakes on one side and turn to finish cooking. Serve immediately with green salad.

Oven-Baked Cod Fillets

cod fillets
milk
salt and pepper
bread crumbs
onions
bay leaves
margarine
bacon strips
lemon juice
lemon slices
parsley

Soak fillets in milk for 2 hours. This bleaches the fish. Drain and wipe dry with a towel. Season with salt and pepper. Dredge in fine bread crumbs. In a greased casserole put a layer of fillets; add onions, bay leaves and margarine. Arrange layer over layer, spread bread crumbs over the fish and top with bacon strips and lemon juice. Bake at 350°F for approximately 30 minutes or until fish loses its transparency. Serve garnished with lemon slices and parsley.

Meat Paté à l'Acadienne

5 lbs pork meat
4 lbs chicken meat
3 onions
2 tbsp pickling spice, finely ground (remove any large ginger roots, etc.
2 cups mashed potato, freshly cooked
1 cup bread crumbs
1 tbsp summer savory
salt and pepper to taste

Remove excess fat and skin from meat. Chop meat into chunks. Place in pot containing 2 cups boiling, salted water. Add 2 onions and pickling spices (tied in a cheesecloth bag). Cook slowly. Cool. With your hands, reduce pieces of meat in size but leave in solid form (never use a blender). Add mashed potato, bread crumbs, 1 onion (finely chopped), summer savory, salt and pepper. Mix this meat mixture with your hands, or a wooden palette. Cover with foil and keep this filling in a 200°F oven while you prepare the crust dough on the baking sheet.

Paté Dough
9 cups flour
¾ lb shortening
2 pkg active dry yeast
3 cups medium hot water
salt
1 egg

Blend flour and shortening. Dissolve the dry yeast as directed on the envelope. Add 1 tsp sugar. When yeast is dissolved, add it to the beaten egg. Combine hot water and flour mixture, then add the yeast and egg mixture. Knead well. Let dough rise. When double in bulk, punch down and let rise again. Roll pieces of dough ¼ inch thick on floured board. Fit into a pie plate. Add about 2 cups of filling for each paté. Cover with top crust. Cut slits and flute the edges as for a pie. Bake in 350°F oven.
Note: As you would have to reheat the meat pies if you serve the pies later, bake only until the crust turns a golden colour.

Rhubarb Pudding

¼ cup sugar
3 tbsp butter
¼ cup milk
½ cup bran flakes or any cereal
½ cup flour
1 tsp baking powder
4 cups diced rhubarb

Cream together sugar, butter and milk. Mix in the dry ingredients. Add rhubarb. Grease casserole. Pour in above mixture.

Topping
½ cup sugar
1 tsp cornstarch

Mix together and sprinkle over the pudding.

Glaze: Pour ½ cup boiling water over the mixture and bake at 350°F for 40 minutes. Serve with whipped cream or ice cream.

Cherry Squares

1 cup sugar
½ cup butter
½ cup milk
1 cup graham cracker crumbs
1 cup walnuts, chopped
1 cup coconut
1 cup glacé cherries
18 graham crackers

Bring sugar, butter and milk to the boiling point. Remove from heat. Add graham cracker crumbs, walnuts, coconut and cherries. Line a 9 x 9-inch square pan with 9 whole graham crackers. Pour filling over crackers and cover with 9 more whole crackers. Refrigerate. Ice with a mixture of unsweetened baking chocolate, icing sugar and milk. Top with graham cracker crumbs.

Sugar Cookies à l'Acadienne

½ cup shortening
2 tbsp butter
1 cup white sugar
1 tsp soda
½ cup milk
2 tsp cream of tartar
1½ cups flour (add more flour as necessary to make a soft dough)
1 egg
nutmeg or vanilla
salt
1½ cups cut-up raisins

Cream shortening and butter until light. Beat in sugar. Dissolve soda in milk. Mix cream of tartar into flour. Add egg, milk, salt, nutmeg or vanilla and raisins to creamed mixture. Add enough flour to make dough easy to handle but not stiff. Turn onto cutting board and, instead of kneading, fold dough over gently with the palm of your hand. This makes a flaky texture. Cut into desired shapes. Bake at 350°F until golden. Do not overbake.

Orange Squares

½ cup shortening
1 cup sugar
1 egg
1 cup sour milk
2 cups flour
½ tsp salt
1 tsp baking powder
1 tsp soda (scant)
grated rind and juice of 1 orange
1 cup walnuts, finely chopped
1 cup dates, cut up
2 cups icing sugar
1 to 2 tbsp butter

Cream together shortening, sugar and egg. Sift flour with salt, baking powder and soda. Add milk and flour alternately to creamed mixture. Add walnuts and dates to mixture. Bake in 8 x 12-inch pan at 350°F. Cool and spread the icing.

Icing: Add the orange rind and as much juice as needed to the icing sugar to make a spreading consistency. Add butter or shortening and a dash of salt. Sprinkle finely chopped walnuts on top of icing.

Easy Party Punch

1 can orange juice
1 can pineapple juice
1 can grapefruit juice
2 cups black tea
½ cup white sugar
2 bottles ginger ale

Combine juices; pour over ice in a large punch bowl. Add ginger ale just before serving. Garnish as you wish with lemon slices or other fruit.

Mustard Bean Pickles

2 lbs white bush beans (Puregold Vesey's)
¼ cup dry mustard
3 cups white sugar
½ cup flour
1 tbsp turmeric (scant)
2 tsp salt
1 tbsp celery seed
2½ cups white vinegar, diluted with ½ cup water

Wash and cut the beans in about 1-inch lengths and cook them in salted water until crisp (but not well-done). Drain. In another bowl combine the mustard, sugar, flour, turmeric, celery seed and salt. Add this to the diluted vinegar in a preserving kettle. Cook, stirring constantly, until thickened. Bring to a boil. Add the beans. Simmer for five minutes more, being careful not to boil this mixture. Ladle into sterilized jars and seal.

Asia

Fish Soup *(Vietnam)*

1 lb white fish fillets
1½ tsp grated fresh ginger
¼ cup fish sauce
½ tsp salt
¼ tsp black pepper
2 small onions, sliced
1 clove garlic, minced
2 tbsp oil
1 tsp turmeric
1 tsp dried shrimp paste
1½ tsp grated lemon rind
8 cups water
1 cup soaked cellophane noodles
2 tbsp chopped scallions
2 tbsp sesame seeds

Cut fish in small pieces and mix with ginger, half the fish sauce, salt and pepper. Marinate ½ hour. Sauté onions and garlic in oil until onions are transparent. Add fish, turmeric and shrimp paste. Cook 3 minutes. Stir in lemon rind, water, drained noodles and rest of fish sauce. Bring to a boil, reduce heat and simmer 10 minutes. Garnish with chopped scallions and sesame seeds. *Serves 6.*

Cauliflower Soup *(Indonesia)*

6 cups beef stock
¼ tsp black pepper
¼ tsp ground mace
¼ tsp ground nutmeg
1½ tsp ground coriander
½ tsp ground cumin
1 small onion, minced
1 clove garlic, minced
1 lb cauliflower, cut in florets

Mix beef stock with ground spices and simmer 10 minutes. Add onion and garlic and continue to simmer for an additional 10 minutes. Stir in cauliflower and cook until just tender. Be careful not to overcook.
Serves 4.

Spring Rolls *(Singapore)*

6 dried or 12 fresh mushrooms
3 tbsp oil
2 tbsp sesame oil
2 cloves garlic, minced
1 tsp grated fresh ginger
½ lb boned pork
½ lb raw shrimp
2½ cups shredded Chinese cabbage
10 water chestnuts, chopped
¾ cup shredded white radish
2 medium onions, chopped
¼ lb bean sprouts
1 cup bamboo shoots, chopped
1½ tbsp soy sauce
1½ tsp salt
1 tbsp cornstarch
2 tbsp water
20 spring roll wrappers (or 40 egg roll wrappers)
oil for frying

Soak dried mushrooms for ½ hour in enough water to cover. Drain, remove stalks and chop. Heat oils in large skillet or wok and sauté garlic and ginger for 1 minute. Finely chop pork and shelled, de-veined shrimp. Add to garlic and stir-fry until meat is cooked. Add vegetables, soy sauce and salt. Mix thoroughly. Blend cornstarch with water, stir into mixture and cook until thickened. Remove from heat and cool. Spoon a couple of tbsp of mixture onto one end of wrapper. Wet edges, roll up and press to seal. Heat oil for deep frying. Cook 1 or 2 rolls at a time, until golden. Drain.
Serves 20.

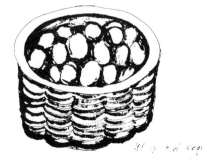

Deep Fried Split Pea Balls *(Burma)*

1 cup split peas
3 small onions, minced
1 green chili, chopped
¼ tsp chili powder
½ tsp ground turmeric
1 tsp salt
oil for deep frying

Cover split peas with water and soak overnight. Drain. Blend until smooth. Pour into bowl. Add onions, chili, chili powder, turmeric and salt. Mix well and form into small balls. Heat oil and drop in balls, one at a time. Cook until golden. Drain well and serve immediately.
Serves 4.

Shrimp and Vegetable Fritters *(Philippines)*

½ lb shrimp
1 cup flour
½ cup ground rice
¼ cup cornstarch
1 cup water
2 eggs
½ tsp black pepper
¾ cup grated raw sweet potato
1 cup fresh bean sprouts
½ cup chopped scallions
oil for deep frying

Shell and de-vein shrimp. Chop in small bits. Mix flour, rice and cornstarch. Combine water with eggs and pepper. Add to flour mixture and beat until smooth. Stir in shrimp, sweet potato, bean sprouts and scallions. Heat oil and drop fritter mixture into it by spoonfuls. Cook until golden, turning occasionally. Drain well and serve immediately.

Spinach *(Korea)*

2 lb fresh spinach
¼ lb pork filet
2 cloves garlic, minced
1 tbsp chopped scallions
2 tbsp peanut oil
3 tbsp soy sauce
½ tsp black pepper
½ cup chopped scallions
2 eggs, beaten
2 tbsp toasted sesame seeds

Remove white stems from spinach. Wash, drain and break into large pieces. Finely chop pork and sauté in oil with garlic and 1 tbsp scallions until meat is cooked. Add spinach, soy sauce and pepper. Mix well, cover and cook until spinach is limp. Stir in ½ cup scallions and eggs. Cook for a few minutes. Sprinkle with sesame seeds and serve.
Serves 6.

Fish with Tomatoes *(Thailand)*

1½ lb white fish fillets
⅓ cup oil
1 small onion, chopped
2 cups chopped tomatoes
3 tbsp lemon juice
salt and pepper
2 red chilies, chopped
3 tbsp flaked coconut

Sauté onion in oil until golden. Add tomatoes, lemon juice, salt and pepper to taste, and chilies. Cover and simmer until tomatoes are very soft. Add fish, cover and cook over low heat until fish is tender. Serve garnished with flaked coconut.

Fish and Rice Casserole *(Malaysia)*

2 lb white fish fillets
¼ cup lemon juice
1½ tsp salt
½ tsp black pepper
1 tsp turmeric
vegetable oil
3 onions, chopped
4 cloves garlic, minced
2 tsp grated fresh ginger
2 tsp ground coriander
1½ tsp ground cumin
⅔ cup chopped tomatoes
¾ cup water

Rice
2 tbsp oil
2 small onions, chopped
4 cardamom pods, slightly crushed
5 whole cloves
½ tsp ground cinnamon
2½ cups white rice
3¾ cups chicken stock
2½ tsp salt

Cut fish into large chunks. Mix lemon juice, salt, pepper and turmeric. Coat fish and set aside for ½ hour. Fry fish in hot oil until golden. Sauté onions, garlic and ginger in 1½ tsp oil until onions are golden. Stir in coriander and cumin and cook 2 minutes. Add tomatoes and water. Simmer covered, until tomatoes are very soft. Add fish, stir; cover and cook 5 minutes. Remove from heat.

Rice: Sauté onions in oil until golden. Add spices and cook 2 minutes. Stir in rice and cook 3 minutes. Add stock and salt, mix well, cover and cook over low heat until stock is absorbed and rice is tender, approximately 15 minutes. Remove cardamom pods and cloves. Layer fish and rice alternately in an oiled baking dish, beginning and ending with rice. Bake at 325°F for ½ hour.
Serves 6 to 8.

Filipino Chicken *(Philippines)*

2 small onions, chopped
4 cloves garlic, minced
2 tbsp oil
3 lb chicken pieces
1½ cups chopped tomatoes
2 tsp salt
½ tsp black pepper
2 cups chicken stock
1 lb small, new potatoes
2 sweet green or red peppers, chopped

Sauté onions and garlic in oil until onions are golden. Add chicken pieces and brown on all sides. Stir in tomatoes, salt, pepper and stock. Bring to boil, reduce heat, cover and cook over medium heat ½ hour. Add potatoes and peppers and continue cooking until chicken and potatoes are tender.
Serves 4 to 6.

Pork Adobo *(Philippines)*

10 cloves garlic, peeled and chopped
1½ cups vinegar
1½ cups water
2 tsp salt
1 tsp black pepper
3 bay leaves
8 pork chops
3 tbsp olive oil

Make marinade by combining garlic, vinegar, water, salt, pepper and bay leaves. Add chops and mix well. Marinate for 2 hours. Transfer to a saucepan and bring to boil, reduce heat and simmer 45 minutes or until pork is tender. Remove meat. Boil marinade until it is reduced by half and thickens. Heat olive oil in skillet and brown chops well. Place meat on serving platter and strain sauce over chops.
Serves 8.

Sesame Beef *(Vietnam)*

¾ lb flank steak
1 tsp salt
½ tsp baking soda
3 tbsp hot water
1½ tbsp soy sauce
2 cloves garlic, minced
¼ cup peanut oil
⅔ cup beef stock
1 tbsp cornstarch
3 tbsp water
3 tsp peanut butter
½ tsp sesame oil
1 tsp chili sauce
1 tbsp toasted sesame seeds

Cut steak in very thin slices. Mix together salt, baking soda, hot water and soy sauce. Blend with steak and marinate for 3 hours. Sauté garlic in oil for 1 minute. Add meat and cook over high heat, stirring constantly, for 3 minutes. Pour on stock, mix well and bring to boil. Thicken with a mixture of cornstarch and water. Remove from heat. Mix peanut butter with sesame oil and add to meat along with chili sauce. Garnish with sesame seeds. *Serves 4.*

River market boat

Almond Cookies *(Singapore)*

½ cup butter
½ cup sugar
1 tsp almond extract
1¼ cups flour
¼ cup ground almonds
blanched whole almonds
1 egg yolk
1 tbsp water

Cream butter and sugar until light and fluffy. Add almond extract and mix well. Mix flour and ground almonds. Gradually add to the creamed mixture. (Mixture will be crumbly.) Form into balls and press slightly. Place on greased baking sheet and press an almond into the top of each cookie. Mix together egg yolk and water and brush top of cookies. Bake at 325°F for about ½ hour.

Coconut Pudding *(Burma)*

1 cup semolina
3 cups thick coconut milk*
1¼ cups sugar
½ cup butter
⅛ tsp salt
½ tsp ground cardamom
4 eggs, separated
¼ cup sesame seeds

Put semolina in top of double boiler and slowly add coconut milk. Stir in sugar and place pot over simmering water. Cook, stirring frequently, until mixture thickens. Add butter a bit at a time, stirring well after each addition. Continue cooking until very thick. Remove from heat. Add salt and cardamom. Add egg yolks one at a time, beating well after each addition. Beat egg whites until stiff and gently fold into the mixture. Pour into well-buttered baking dish and sprinkle with sesame seeds. Bake at 325°F for about 1 hour or until lightly browned. Serve warm or cold.

*To make coconut milk, pour 5 cups very hot water over 4 cups flaked coconut. Allow to stand 15 minutes and strain through a fine sieve or piece of muslin.

China

Noodle Soup

1 cup cellophane noodles
6 cups chicken stock
1 tsp salt
½ lb ground pork
½ tsp grated fresh ginger
1½ tbsp chopped water chestnuts
1 tsp cornstarch
3 tsp soy sauce
1 tbsp chopped scallions

Soak noodles for ½ hour in enough cold water to cover. Drain well and cut into 4-inch lengths. Bring stock and salt to a boil. Add noodles and cook 15 minutes. Blend together pork, ginger, chestnuts, cornstarch and soy sauce. Form into small balls and drop into boiling soup. Continue to cook for an additional 10 minutes, or until pork balls are done. Serve garnished with chopped scallions.
Serves 4.

Watercress Soup

¼ lb lean pork
1½ tsp cornstarch
½ tsp sugar
½ tsp black pepper
1½ tbsp soy sauce
1½ tbsp vegetable oil
1 tsp grated fresh ginger
2 tsp salt
6 cups boiling water
½ lb watercress

Cut pork into very thin slices. Mix with cornstarch, sugar, pepper, soy sauce and 1 tbsp oil. Set aside. Heat remaining oil, add ginger and salt and sauté 1 minute. Add boiling water and return to a boil. Stir in watercress, cover and simmer 5 minutes. Slowly stir in pork. Replace the lid and simmer 15 minutes.
Serves 6.

Green Onion Pancakes

Batter
4 cups flour
1½ cups water
½ lb green onions, finely chopped
oil for frying

Filling
3 tbsp chopped green onion
1 tbsp lard
1 tsp salt

Mix together flour, water and green onions to form a soft dough. Add a little more water if necessary. Divide into six equal parts. Roll each portion very thinly into an oblong shape. Mix together ingredients for the filling and divide into six portions. Place one portion of filling on each pancake. Roll up and coil to form a flat cake. Roll lightly with rolling pin to about 6 inches in diameter. Heat oil and fry over medium heat for 2 minutes on each side. Reduce heat and fry for an additional 3 minutes on each side or until golden brown.
Serves 6.

Stuffed Steamed Bread

Bread
1 tbsp dried yeast
2½ tbsp sugar
½ tsp salt
2 cups flour
½ cup warm water

Filling
1½ lb pork shoulder
1 tbsp cooking wine
2 tbsp sugar
½ tbsp salt
1 tbsp soy sauce
1 tbsp hoi-sin sauce or barbecue sauce
3 cloves garlic
1 tbsp salted black bean
2 tbsp oil
2 tbsp dark soy sauce
2 tbsp sugar
½ cup water
1½ tbsp cornstarch

Bread: Mix together yeast, sugar, salt and flour in a large bowl. Make a well in centre and add warm water. Mix to form a soft dough. Knead for 10 minutes on floured board. Return to bowl, cover and let rise in a warm place until doubled. Knead lightly and let rise again. Roll into a long rope 1½ inches in diameter. Cut into 1-inch pieces and roll into ovals 4 inches long. Dust one side with flour and double over. Set aside for 15 minutes or until doubled. Cook in a steamer for 10 to 15 minutes or until light and spongy.

Filling: Cut pork into large, long pieces. Marinate for 1 hour in a mixture of wine, sugar, salt, 1 tbsp soy sauce and hoi-sin sauce. Bake at 500°F for 20 minutes. Dice cooked pork into small cubes. Mash garlic and black bean together and brown in 2 tbsp oil. Add pork. Stir in dark soy sauce and sugar. Blend cornstarch with water and add. Cook until mixture thickens. Remove from heat. Fill steamed bread with pork filling and serve.

Fried Rice

3 tbsp oil
few frozen shrimp, diced (optional)
½ cup chopped green onions
1 cup diced celery
1 cup sliced mushrooms
2½ cups cold, cooked rice
2 tbsp soy sauce
5-spice powder
salt
1 egg, slightly beaten

Heat oil in large pan or wok. Sauté shrimp, onions and celery in oil until almost tender (3 minutes). Add mushrooms, rice and soy sauce. Season to taste with 5-spice powder and a little salt. Cook on low heat for 10 minutes, stirring occasionally. Stir in egg and continue to cook, just until egg is done.

Braised Mushrooms and Bamboo Shoots

¼ lb dried mushrooms
16-oz can bamboo shoots
oil for frying
4 slices fresh ginger
2 tsp salt
1 tsp sugar
¼ cup water
1 tsp sesame oil
1 tbsp cornstarch

Soak mushrooms in 3 cups water for ½ hour. Drain, reserving liquid. Cut bamboo shoots into thick slices. Heat 2 tbsp oil and sauté ginger until golden. Add mushrooms and bamboo shoots. Cook for 1 minute. Stir in reserved liquid, salt and sugar. Cover and cook over medium heat for 30 minutes. Blend together water, sesame oil and cornstarch and stir into mushroom mixture. Cook, stirring constantly, until sauce is thick and clear.
Serves 4.

Bean Curd with Shrimp

1 cake bean curd, as fresh as possible
1 can chicken broth
few fresh mushrooms, sliced
few frozen shrimp, thawed and sliced
salt and pepper to taste
1 tsp cornstarch
1 tbsp water

Cut bean curd into pieces 1 inch square and ½ inch thick. Heat broth, add bean curd, mushrooms and shrimp. Season to taste. Mix cornstarch with water. Add to broth to thicken.

Rice with Chicken Sauce

3 cups hot cooked rice
1 chicken breast
1 tbsp dry sherry
1 tbsp soy sauce
½ tsp sugar
pinch of pepper
1 tsp cornstarch
1 egg white
1 tsp grated fresh ginger
oil for frying
2 tsp cornstarch
¾ cup water
1 tsp salt
1 egg, beaten
2 scallions, chopped

Skin and bone chicken. Chop meat finely. Make marinade with sherry, soy sauce, sugar, pepper, 1 tsp cornstarch and egg white. Add chicken and set aside for ½ hour. Heat 2 tbsp oil and sauté ginger for 1 minute. Add chicken mixture and cook until meat turns white. Mix together 2 tsp cornstarch, water and salt and add to chicken. Cook until clear and thickened, stirring constantly. Stir in egg and remove from heat. Pour chicken sauce over rice and garnish with chopped scallions.
Serves 4.

Stuffed Fish

3 lb whole white fish
2½ tbsp dried shrimp
10 dried Chinese mushrooms
5 scallions, chopped
3 tbsp chopped water chestnuts
3 tsp fish sauce
¼ cup peanut oil

Sauce
1½ tsp soy sauce
¼ cup dry sherry
¾ cup water
1 tbsp sugar
1 tsp grated fresh ginger
3 tsp cornstarch
1 tbsp water

Clean and scale fish, leaving on head and tail. Scrub inside with salt. Rinse and wipe dry. Soak shrimp and mushrooms separately in enough hot water to cover, for ½ hour. Drain. Finely chop shrimp. Discard mushroom stems and finely chop caps. Mix together shrimp, mushrooms, scallions, chestnuts, fish sauce and all but 1 tbsp peanut oil. Blend thoroughly. Stuff fish with this mixture and secure the opening with skewers. Brush fish with remaining oil. Bake at 350°F for about ½ hour or until fish is tender. Blend soy sauce, sherry, water, sugar and ginger in a saucepan. Bring to a boil. Reduce heat and simmer 5 minutes. Mix cornstarch with water and add to sauce, stirring constantly until mixture thickens. Place fish on serving platter and pour on hot sauce.
Serves 6.

Mussels, Cantonese Style

2 lb mussels, in shells
8 tbsp oil
½ cup chopped green onions
½ tbsp chopped fresh ginger
6 cloves garlic, minced
4 tbsp oyster sauce
1 tbsp soy sauce
1 tbsp sugar
2 tbsp cooking sherry
2½ tbsp cornstarch
1 cup cold water

Rinse and drain mussels. Heat 4 tbsp oil and sauté onions, ginger and garlic. Remove from heat. Add oyster sauce, soy sauce, sugar and sherry. Return to heat. Dissolve cornstarch in water and add to sauce. Stir until smooth and bubbling. Remove from heat; keep hot. Heat 4 tbsp oil in large pot or wok. Add mussels all at once. Cover and cook until shells are partly open. Drain liquid. Add prepared sauce. Cover and continue to cook until shells are completely open.

Variation: Lobster may be substituted for the mussels. Chop lobster into 1½-inch pieces, in the shell, and proceed as above. It is advisable to do this messy chopping outside, on a picnic table covered with newspaper.

Fried Noodles with Chicken

½ lb cooked chicken meat
3 bamboo shoots
¼ lb fresh mushrooms
½ lb egg noodles
oil for frying
1 tsp salt
½ tsp sesame oil
chopped scallions

Cut meat into small pieces. Thinly slice bamboo shoots and mushrooms. Cook noodles in boiling, salted water until tender. Drain well. Fry noodles in a little hot oil for 2 minutes, stirring constantly. Remove from pan and keep warm. Sauté chicken in the oiled pan for about 3 minutes. Add bamboo shoots, mushrooms, salt and sesame oil. Cook for 3 minutes, stirring occasionally. Pour over fried noodles and garnish with scallions.
Serves 4.

Beef with Sweet Green Peppers

1 lb lean beef
1 tsp cornstarch
1 tsp soy sauce
¼ cup oil
1 tsp salt
¼ tsp black pepper
1 scallion, chopped
1 clove garlic, minced
3 sweet green peppers, sliced
2 stalks celery, sliced
3 tsp cornstarch
½ cup water
2 tsp soy sauce

Cut beef into thin slices. Marinate with 1 tsp cornstarch and 1 tsp soy sauce. Sauté beef in oil with salt and pepper for 1 minute. Add scallion, garlic, green peppers and celery. Cook for 2 minutes. Add 2 tbsp water, cover and cook an additional 2 minutes. Blend cornstarch with water and soy sauce, until smooth. Add to beef, mix well and cook until thickened.
Serves 4.

Fried Liver

1 lb calf liver
3 tsp cornstarch
2½ tbsp dry sherry
1½ tsp grated fresh ginger
1 medium onion
¼ lb fresh mushrooms
½ lb bamboo shoots
2 tbsp vegetable oil
2 tsp sesame oil
1 tbsp soy sauce

Cut liver into thin slices. Mix with cornstarch, sherry and ginger.
Slice onion, mushrooms and bamboo shoots. Heat oils in skillet
and quickly fry liver and vegetables over high heat, stirring constantly. Fry until meat is just cooked. Do not overcook. Add soy
sauce, mix thoroughly and serve immediately.
Serves 4.

Fried Sliced Chicken

1 lb raw white chicken meat
¼ lb green beans
½ sweet green pepper
¼ lb fresh mushrooms
1 medium onion
1 clove garlic
2 tsp vegetable oil
salt and pepper
1 tbsp dry sherry
½ tsp sugar

Slice chicken thinly; coat each piece with oil and set aside. Slice
beans and boil for 2 minutes in salted water. Drain. Slice green
pepper, mushrooms and onion. Sauté whole garlic in 2 tsp oil
for 1 minute. Remove garlic and add green pepper, mushrooms
and onion. Season to taste with salt and pepper. Sauté until
onion is transparent. Remove vegetables and keep warm. In
same skillet, cook chicken until tender. Add vegetables, sherry
and sugar. Mix well and heat through.
Serves 4.

Chicken and Almonds

1 lb chicken
⅓ cup vegetable oil
1 cup blanched almonds
¼ lb fresh mushrooms
1 sweet green pepper
2 bamboo shoots
1 medium onion
2 tsp salt
2 tsp cornstarch
2 tsp sugar
1 tbsp soy sauce
1 tbsp dry sherry
1¼ cups water

Cut chicken into small cubes. Heat 1 tbsp oil and sauté almonds until golden. Remove from oil. Chop mushrooms, pepper, bamboo shoots and onion. Heat 2 tbsp oil and sauté onion until golden. Add chicken and fry until meat is slightly brown. Stir in vegetables with 1 tsp salt and the rest of the oil. Cook over medium heat for 5 minutes, stirring constantly. In a small saucepan, blend together the remaining salt, cornstarch, sugar, soy sauce and sherry. Slowly add water and bring to a boil, stirring constantly. Pour over chicken. Add almonds and heat through. *Serves 4.*

Germany

Lobster Cocktail

1 lb lobster meat, fresh or frozen
lemon juice
2 tbsp finely chopped parsley
2 cups mayonnaise
1 tbsp tomato paste
½ cup whipping cream
salt and pepper
6 each red and green maraschino cherries, halved
1 hard-boiled egg, sliced
1 tsp cognac (optional)

Break lobster meat into bite-sized pieces. Sprinkle with lemon juice. In a separate bowl, combine parsley, mayonnaise, tomato paste, whipping cream, salt and pepper until smooth and pink. Stir in cherries, egg and cognac. Add lobster meat and mix carefully. Serve on a bed of lettuce leaves, with toast and butter. *Serves 4.*

Grandma's Lentil Soup

1 lb brown lentils
4 tbsp finely chopped bacon
1 onion, chopped
salt and pepper
1 carrot, chopped
2 cups water
1 cup raw potato cubes
½ cup dry red wine
4 slices smoked picnic ham, cubed

Wash lentils in hot water and drain. In a casserole, brown the bacon, then add onion, salt and pepper, carrot and water. Bring to a boil; add lentils and potato cubes; cover and cook 1½ hours. Add water when needed, simmer again and add wine. Add ham just before serving.
Serves 4.

German Omelette (*Bauernfrühstück*)

½ cup butter or margarine
2 cups diced, raw potatoes
1 cup finely chopped onion
¾ tsp salt
dash pepper
1 cup diced ham
chopped parsley
6 eggs
2 tbsp milk
½ cup shredded cheese

Melt butter in frying pan. Add potatoes, onion and part of the seasoning. Cook over medium heat, stirring occasionally to brown evenly, until potatoes are tender. Add ham, cook slightly longer and sprinkle with parsley. Reduce heat. Beat eggs with balance of seasoning and milk. Pour over potato mixture. Sprinkle with cheese. Cover until cheese melts.
Serves 4 to 6.

Potato Dumplings *(Kartoffel Knoedel)*

900 g potatoes
30 g butter
2 eggs
120 g flour
120 g cream of wheat
½ tsp salt
dash nutmeg

Cook and peel potatoes. Press through potato press or meat grinder. Add all other ingredients. Mix, shape dough into balls and put into boiling, salted water. Cook for about 10 minutes until balls float to the surface. Lift out. Serve with sauerbraten and red cabbage.
Serves 4.

Red Cabbage with Red Wine

1 medium red cabbage
salt and pepper
2 tbsp shortening or lard
1 apple, peeled
1 onion minced
1 to 2 bay leaves
3 cloves
1 tbsp sugar
¾ cup water
¾ cup dry red wine
1 tbsp white vinegar

Shred cabbage; sprinkle with salt and pepper. Melt shortening or lard in a skillet. Add cabbage, cover tightly and steam over low heat until soft. Slice apple thinly. Add apple, onion, bay leaves, cloves, sugar, water and wine. Simmer for 15 minutes. Before serving, add vinegar. Only then will you have a bright red cabbage. If desired, 1 tsp cornstarch dissolved in a little water may be added. Serve with pork roast and creamed potatoes or potato dumplings.
Serves 4 to 6.

Potato Pancakes *(Kartoffelpuffer or Reibekuchen)*

1 kg potatoes
6 g salt
1 small onion, grated
1 to 2 eggs
20 to 30 g flour or bread crumbs
80 to 100 g oil or fat for frying

Peel and grate potatoes. Add salt, onions, egg and flour or bread crumbs. Heat oil or fat in frying pan. Spoon batter on heated fat (about 2 tbsp for each pancake). Press flat and brown on each side. Serve with applesauce, salad or cottage cheese.

Sauerkraut Stuffing for Roast Goose

2½ lb sauerkraut
1 cup white wine
½ tsp freshly ground black pepper
1 tsp caraway seed
1 large onion, cut in eighths
2 tbsp butter
1 large potato, peeled
2 unpeeled apples, cored

Put sauerkraut, wine, pepper and caraway in a heavy saucepan. Cover and simmer 1 hour. Add water if necessary. Put onion in blender, cover with cold water and coarsely chop. Drain well and sauté in butter until lightly browned. Add to sauerkraut. Chop potato and apple into 1-inch cubes. Add to sauerkraut and mix well. Cool before stuffing goose.
Yield: stuffing for 8 to 10 lb goose.

Sauerbraten with Dumplings

3½ to 4 lb beef chuck roast
2 onions, sliced
2 bay leaves
12 peppercorns
6 whole cloves
12 juniper berries
2 tsp salt
1½ cups red wine vinegar
1 cup boiling water
2 tbsp shortening
2 to 3 lb red cabbage, cut into 8 or 10 wedges
12 gingersnaps, crushed
2 tsp sugar
caraway dumpling dough (see below)

Place meat in glass dish. Mix onions, bay leaves, peppercorns, cloves, juniper berries, salt, vinegar and water; pour over meat. Cover tightly; refrigerate 3 days, turning meat 6 times. Remove meat and reserve marinade. Melt shortening in large skillet and brown meat. Add reserved marinade. Cover tightly; simmer 2½ to 3 hours or until meat is tender. Remove meat and onions; keep warm. Strain liquid and drippings into skillet; measure and add water to make 2½ cups liquid. Add cabbage; cover and simmer 10 minutes. Stir in gingersnaps and sugar; simmer 3 minutes. Prepare dumpling dough, drop by spoonfuls onto cabbage. Cook uncovered over low heat for 10 minutes, cover and cook for an additional 10 minutes. Serve meat, vegetables and dumplings on a platter; accompany with gravy.

Caraway Dumpling Dough: Mix together 2 cups biscuit mix, ⅔ cup milk and 1½ tsp caraway seed.

Wine Marinade for Sauerbraten or Sweet and Sour Meat

¾ litre dry white or red wine
2 small carrots, diced
1 medium onion, cut in rings
1 to 2 bay leaves
4 to 6 kernels of allspice or whole allspice
5 whole cloves

Combine all ingredients; boil for about 2 to 3 minutes; pour over meat; turn once. Cover; cool; set in refrigerator at least 12 hours.

Liver Dumplings "Bavaria"

6 day-old buns
¾ cup lukewarm milk
1 lb beef liver
6 strips bacon
1 onion, finely chopped
2 eggs
2 tbsp chopped parsley
1 tsp marjoram
3 tbsp bread crumbs
salt and pepper

Cut buns into pieces and soak in lukewarm milk. Meanwhile, grind up liver and bacon. Mix with onion, eggs, parsley, marjoram, bread crumbs, salt and pepper. Add bun mixture and knead until smooth. Let rest for 30 minutes. With wet hands form dumplings (golf-ball size). Simmer in salted water for 15 minutes. Serve with sauerkraut and creamed potatoes, or in clear broth.
Hint—Before cooking liver, place it in milk for a while. This makes the liver tastier and more tender.

Kohlrabi-Eintopf

Meatballs
250 g hamburger
salt and pepper
10 mL paprika
1 egg
1 small onion, chopped
30 mL bread crumbs

Mix all ingredients together. Form into meatballs and cook in boiling water for 10 minutes.

Stew
4 kohlrabi
2 cups leeks
40 g butter
300 g frozen peas
1½ litres chicken broth
salt and pepper
pinch sugar
2 sprigs parsley

Peel and quarter kohlrabi, then slice thinly. Cut leeks into thick rings. Steam kohlrabi in butter for a few minutes. Add peas and leeks. Steam for another few minutes. Add broth, salt, pepper and sugar. Simmer for 20 minutes. Just before serving, add meatballs and parsley. Heat through for 5 minutes; serve.

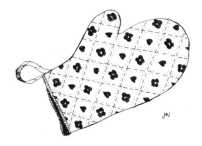

Franconian Beef Roll *(Rouladen)*

1 boneless round steak
salt and pepper
bacon strips
2 breakfast or Oktoberfest sausages
1 egg
1 tbsp bread crumbs
1 tsp marjoram
1½ onions, finely chopped
2 tbsp butter
1 cup boiling water
½ cup dry red wine
½ tbsp cornstarch

Sprinkle steak with salt and pepper, cover with bacon strips and set aside. Remove skin from sausages and combine with egg, bread crumbs, marjoram and ½ onion. Spread carefully over bacon strips and roll up steak carefully. Fasten with household string. In a heavy skillet, melt butter and quickly brown meat on all sides. Arrange remaining onion around the meat. Stir until golden to deep brown. Lower heat, pour boiling water around roll, cover tightly and simmer 2 hours. Add wine, bring to a boil and remove from heat. Dissolve cornstarch in a little cold water. Add to liquid in pot and return to a boil to thicken.
Serves 4.

Cabbage Rolls *(Kohlrollen)*

1 cabbage
60 g fat or bacon
¼ to ½ litre water or broth
1 tbsp flour
salt

Filling
150 to 250 g ground beef or pork, or meat leftovers
30 g lean bacon
1 dry or day-old bun, or
    2 to 3 cooked potatoes, grated
1 onion, chopped
1 egg
salt and pepper

Blanch cabbage in boiling, salted water. Cool and separate leaves. Mix together meat, bun or potatoes, onion, egg, salt and pepper for filling. Place filling on cabbage leaves and roll up, folding in sides while rolling. Secure with thread or string. Heat fat or bacon, place rolls in pan and brown on all sides. Add water or broth; simmer for about 45 minutes. Mix flour with some cold water and add to liquid in pan to make gravy. Chopped tomatoes may be added after rolls are browned. Season to taste with salt and pepper.

German Christmas Cake *(Christstollen)*

3 tbsp yeast
2 lb all-purpose flour
½ lb butter or margarine
3 tbsp oil
dash salt
2 tbsp white sugar
2 eggs
½ litre lukewarm milk
7 oz marzipan/almond paste (optional)
1 cup ground almonds
1 tsp cinnamon
½ tsp cardamom
dash mace
½ cup white rum
1½ cup raisins
1½ cup currants
½ cup candied orange peel, chopped
½ cup candied lemon peel, chopped

Dissolve yeast in 3 tbsp lukewarm milk. Finely chop marzipan. Mix together flour, butter, oil, salt, sugar, eggs, milk and marzipan. Add yeast. Stir in nuts, spices and rum. Knead to a soft dough, cover with tea towel and let rise 1½ hours. Knead in raisins, currants and peel. Place on greased baking sheet. Shape dough into an oval, approximately 8 x 10 inches. Brush with soft butter and fold over once, lengthwise, to form the stollen. Let rise 1 hour. Bake at 350°F for 1½ to 2 hours. Sprinkle with icing sugar. This cake should be prepared a month before Christmas in order for the flavour to develop. Wrap in foil and freezer bag. Store in a cool place.

"The shape of the stollen symbolizes the diapers of the Christ child."

Apple Cheese Strudel

Pastry
1 cup sweet butter
½ lb cottage cheese
2 cups flour

Filling
2 cups pie apples
½ cup sugar
1 tsp cinnamon
1 tsp nutmeg
½ cup chopped mixed peel
½ tsp salt
1 egg, beaten
blanched almonds, chopped

Mix butter, cottage cheese and flour in a bowl. Chill for ½ hour.
Roll out to a large oblong (not too thin). Mix apples with sugar,
spices, peel and salt. Spread over pastry. Glaze edges with beaten
egg. Tuck in ends of pastry and fold over. Brush top of roll with
beaten egg and sprinkle with chopped almonds. Bake at 375°F
for 30 to 45 minutes or until golden brown.
Serves 6 to 8.

German Apple Cake

4 green apples, peeled
3 tbsp lemon juice
2 tbsp butter or margarine
6 eggs
1 tsp salt
1 cup flour
1 cup milk
1 tbsp lemon juice
brown sugar

Thinly slice apples and mix with lemon juice. Melt butter in a
large frying pan. Sauté apples for about 5 minutes. Transfer to
baking dish. Beat eggs; add salt, flour and milk, beating constantly. Pour batter over apples and bake in a very hot oven
(450°F) for 20 minutes. Reduce heat to 350°F and bake 10 minutes
longer. Sprinkle with lemon juice and sugar and serve.
Serves 8.

Red Currant Cake *(Schwaebischer Traeubieskuchen)*

Dough
125 g butter or margarine
100 g sugar
250 g flour
2 eggs
grated peel of ½ lemon
1 tsp baking powder

Filling
2 egg whites
75 to 100 g sugar
2 tsp cornstarch
500 g red currants (fresh or canned, or blueberries)

Mix together all ingredients for dough. Roll out and place on a 10-inch cake pan. Press dough up on sides to form a rim. Bake at 325°F for 25 minutes.

Filling: Beat egg whites. Gradually add sugar and cornstarch, and beat until stiff. Fold in currants. Spread on baked crust and bake for an additional 20 minutes. Place cake under grill or broiler for a few seconds until light brown on top.

Peach Kuchen

2 cups flour
¼ tsp baking powder
½ tsp salt
¼ cup sugar
½ cup butter or margarine
6 large peaches
1 tsp cinnamon
2 egg yolks
1 cup sour cream

Sift flour, baking powder, salt and 2 tbsp sugar into a bowl. Cut in butter until mixture resembles fine crumbs. Spread into a buttered 8-inch baking pan and press crumbly pastry on bottom and sides. Peel and slice peaches. Arrange slices over pastry and sprinkle with remaining sugar and cinnamon. Bake at 400°F for 15 minutes. Mix together egg yolks and sour cream; pour over peaches. Bake 30 minutes longer.
Serves 6 to 8.

Linzertorte

200 g butter
200 g sugar
3 eggs
pinch each salt and ground cloves
½ tsp cinnamon
grated peel of ½ lemon
100 g plain cookie crumbs
150 g ground almonds
225 g flour, sifted
350 g raspberry jam
1 egg yolk, beaten

Grease a 25 cm (10-inch) spring-form pan. In a large bowl, cream butter and sugar until light and fluffy. Add 3 eggs, one at a time, with salt, cloves, cinnamon and lemon peel. Mix cookie crumbs and almonds. Stir into egg mixture. Fold in flour to make a soft dough. Cover and refrigerate 2 hours. On a floured surface, roll or pat out ⅔ of dough to a 25 cm (10-inch) round. Leave remaining dough in fridge. Place round of dough in prepared pan so it is about 2 cm (¾ inch) high around the edges. Spread jam over dough. Roll out remaining dough 3 cm (⅛ inch) thick. Cut into ½-inch strips. Arrange in a lattice pattern over the jam. Brush with beaten egg yolk. Bake at 375°F for 35 to 40 minutes. Remove to a rack to cool completely.

Holland

Vegetable Soup *(Groente Soep)*

1 kg beef
10 bouillon cubes
1 bunch celery, chopped
3 carrots, chopped
few pieces cauliflower or leek
10 green beans, chopped
vermicelli or spaghetti
300 g hamburger
salt and nutmeg
2 eggs
2 Dutch rusks

Cut 1 kg beef into bite-sized pieces. Put in soup pot with bouillon cubes, cover well with water and simmer 3 to 4 hours. Add vegetables and vermicelli. Mix hamburger with a little salt and nutmeg. Add eggs and crumbled rusks. Shape into small meatballs. Add to soup and continue to cook for 15 minutes.

Chicken Soup *(Kippensoep)*

1 stewing chicken
10 bouillon cubes
1 bunch celery, finely chopped
1 bunch parsley, finely chopped
vermicelli or spaghetti

Put chicken in soup pot and cover with 4 to 5 litres water, or as much as is necessary to completely cover chicken. Add bouillon cubes and simmer 3 to 4 hours. Remove chicken from pot and take meat off bones. Meanwhile, add celery, parsley and vermicelli to water. Season to taste with salt and pepper and cook for about 20 minutes. Return meat to pot and serve.
Serves 6 to 10.

Meatballs *(Bitterballen)*

1 cup thick white sauce
2 cups chopped, cooked meat (roast beef, ham or combination)
1 tbsp minced parsley
salt and pepper
Worcestershire sauce
fine dry bread crumbs
1 egg
cooking oil

Mix together white sauce, meat, parsley, salt, pepper and Worcestershire sauce to taste. Chill. Shape into 1-inch balls and roll in bread crumbs. Dry for 2 hours. Mix egg with 2 tbsp water. Dip balls in egg and roll again in crumbs. Fry in deep hot fat (400°F) for 1 or 2 minutes. Drain. Serve piping hot on a wooden pick, with mustard as a dip.

Ham and Cheese Savories
(Warme Ham—En Kaassandwiches)

8 thin slices stale bread
4 slices (¼ oz each) cheese (Gouda or Edam)
4 slices ham (½ oz each)
butter or margarine

Remove crusts from bread and cut slices to identical sizes. Trim ham and cheese to match bread. Put one slice each of ham and cheese between two slices of bread. Spread outsides of bread with butter and fry until crisp and golden.

Red Cabbage

1 red cabbage
vinegar

Cut cabbage through the middle first; then put halves on the
cutting board and slice very thin. Put in pan with a little water.
Cook until tender and add a little vinegar. Serve together with
applesauce, as a vegetable with meat and potatoes.

Fried Meat *(Vlees Bakken)*

Meat (pork or beef steak, stewing beef, etc., as much as required
    for serving)
salt, pepper and meat spices
liquid bouillon
butter
3 onions, chopped
4 tomatoes, chopped
½ litre water
1 bay leaf

Cut meat into serving-sized pieces. Season with salt, pepper,
meat spices and bouillon. Let stand a couple of hours or overnight. Heat butter in pan. Brown meat on both sides and remove
from pan. Add onions to pan and fry. Add tomatoes and continue
to fry. Return meat to pan. Add water, a little bouillon and bay
leaf. Simmer 2 hours, adding water if necessary. Remove meat
from pan. Strain liquid and serve as a sauce.

Dutch Spice Cake *(Ontbijtkoek)*

2 cups self-rising flour
½ cup dark brown sugar
⅓ cup molasses
1 cup milk
1 tsp each ground cloves, cinnamon and ginger
½ tsp grated nutmeg
pinch salt

Combine all ingredients to a smooth paste. Butter an 8-inch square cake pan. Fill pan with dough and bake in a slow oven (300°F) for about 1 hour. When cooked, allow to cool and keep in a tin for 24 hours before serving. This cake keeps moist when put in the bread bin with the bread. It is often served buttered, for breakfast, or as a mid-morning snack.

Buttercake *(Boterkoek)*

2 cups flour
1 cup butter
1 cup sugar
1 small egg, beaten
salt
3 oz finely chopped candied ginger

Knead all ingredients into a smooth paste, keeping half the beaten egg for decorating. Butter a pie pan that is 1 inch deep and 8 inches in diameter. Press dough into pan. Brush the rest of the egg on top. Decorate the top in squares with the back of a knife. Bake in a moderate oven (350°F) for 30 minutes or until golden brown. While still hot, press the middle of the cake down with the back of a spoon. Cool. When firm to the touch turn out onto a wire rack. The cake should be soft inside, but done and hard on the outside.

Snowballs *(Sneeuwballen)*

½ cup cold water
1 tsp salt
½ cup butter
10 tbsp flour, sifted
2 eggs
2 tbsp currants or raisins, washed and dried
cooking oil or fat, for frying
sifted icing sugar

Mix water, salt and butter and bring to a boil. Remove from heat and stir in flour. Return to heat. Keep stirring with wooden spoon until mixture leaves the pan and forms a ball. Remove from heat. Cool and then break in the eggs, one at a time, beating well until smooth. Add currants or raisins. Heat oil to 360°F. With a metal spoon heated in the oil, take out a spoonful of batter and fry until golden brown on each side—about 10 minutes. These will puff up and become very light. (Watch the temperature of the oil carefully.) Drain well and sprinkle with icing sugar. These are a traditional New Year's Eve sweet. They may also be made without the fruit, cut open and filled with sweetened whipped cream.

Hungary

Green Bean Sour Cream Soup

3½ cups green beans
½ cup cubed potatoes
1 cup wax beans
½ cup peas
2 tbsp oil
2 tsp flour
1 cup sour cream
1 tsp paprika

Cook vegetables in salted water. Drain, reserving the water. Put oil in soup pot and stir in flour. Add reserved liquid. Cook, stirring constantly until thickened. Add paprika and sour cream. Beat until smooth. Add vegetables and heat through. Add more water or milk if necessary.

Hungarian Pancakes

Hungarian pancakes are served for dinner at noon, or supper—never breakfast. They are cooked until golden (not brown) on a large, level-edged skillet greased with oil or unsalted butter. For an 8-inch pancake, use ¼ cup batter. This is poured onto a hot, greased skillet and the skillet is tipped quickly, to spread batter thinly. When baking filled pancakes in the oven, one unfilled pancake should be spread over the top, to keep in moisture. It should be removed before serving.

Plain Pancakes—Crêpes *(Palacsinta)*

2 cups sifted flour
1 tsp salt
4 eggs, separated
3 cups milk or equal parts milk and water

Combine flour, salt, egg yolks and 1 cup milk, stirring until smooth. Gradually stir in rest of milk to make a batter the consistency of heavy sweet cream. Beat egg whites until stiff but not dry, and fold into the batter. Stir again before dipping each pancake. Cook thin cakes on an 8-inch skillet, tipping to spread batter. Flip over once. May be used with fillings or toppings, as a main dish or dessert. If using for dessert, fruit, jam, honey, syrup or sugar may be used as a filling or sprinkled on top of pancake before heating for 20 minutes at 350°F. Crêpes may be layered with filling up to twelve high and cut as you would a pie to serve, or may be rolled individually, heated and served.

Variations: Add 2 beaten eggs with the first cup of milk. Will be less delicate.

For dessert add ½ tsp salt and 1 tbsp sugar to recipe.

Cottage Cheese Filling *(Túrós Töltelék)*

2 cups cottage cheese
1 egg yolk
2 tbsp sugar
½ cup sour cream
½ cup raisins

Press the cottage cheese through a sieve or mash with a fork until well-creamed. Mix with egg yolk, sugar, cream and raisins. Spread each pancake with 1 tbsp of cheese mixture, roll up, arrange in a baking dish and reheat in a moderate oven (350°F) for 20 minutes.

Mushroom-Filled Pancakes
(Gombával Töltött Palacsinta)

1½ cups finely chopped mushrooms
2 tbsp butter
½ tsp salt
dash pepper
½ cup sour cream
1 egg, slightly beaten
plain pancakes (see page 56)

Brown mushrooms in butter, cool slightly and combine with the salt and pepper, sour cream and egg. Using this filling, proceed in layers of 1 tbsp of filling between each layer of pancake. Butter top layer and heat at 350°F for 20 minutes.

Cucumbers with Sour Cream *(Tejfölös Uborka)*

4 large cucumbers
2 tsp salt
¼ cup vinegar
½ tsp paprika or ⅛ tsp pepper
¼ cup heavy sweet or sour cream
salad oil (optional)

Peel the cucumbers and slice thinly. Sprinkle with salt and let stand 15 minutes. Drain and press out moisture. Add vinegar and paprika. A few minutes before serving, add cream and salad oil (if desired). A little finely chopped onion may be added.
Serves 6.

Lobster-Filled Pancakes *(Rakkal Töltött Palacsinta)*

½ cup finely chopped mushrooms
1 tbsp butter
1 cup cooked lobster or crab meat
1 tbsp chopped parsley
½ tsp salt
dash pepper
½ cup sour cream
1 slice white bread, softened in milk
plain pancakes (see page 56)

Brown mushrooms lightly in butter and let cool. Combine all ingredients. Spread 1 tbsp filling on each pancake. Arrange in buttered baking dish in layers and butter top layer before heating at 350°F for 20 minutes.
Serves 8 to 10.

White Fish Baked in White Wine
(Sült Hal Fehérborban)

3 medium potatoes
2 lb fish fillets
2 tbsp butter
1 cup sour cream
2 cups sliced mushrooms
⅔ cup white wine
1 tsp salt

Thinly slice potatoes and cut fish into serving-sized pieces. Line a buttered baking dish with potato slices. Dot with butter and cover with ½ cup sour cream. Cook mushrooms in wine for 10 minutes and spread in pan. Arrange pieces of fish over mixture, sprinkle with salt and top with remaining cream. Bake at 350°F for 30 minutes or until potatoes are done.
Serves 6.

Goulash *(Gulyás)*

4 lb beef (chuck or rump), cut in 2-inch pieces
2 strips bacon or salt pork, or 2 tbsp bacon fat
6 onions, coarsely chopped
3 tbsp paprika
1½ tsp salt
2 green peppers, coarsely chopped

Brown half of beef in its own fat in a large skillet. Transfer to Dutch oven and repeat with other half. Rinse the skillet with a cup of water and add the liquid to the meat. Cover and cook slowly over low heat. Chop the bacon and fry in skillet; add the onions and brown lightly. Stir in paprika and salt. Combine with the simmering meat. Stir in uncooked green peppers and continue cooking slowly for about 2 hours or until meat is tender — not soft. Serve with noodles.
Serves 8 to 10.

Chicken Paprika with Rice or Dumplings
(Paprikash Csirke)

1 frying chicken, cut up
1 onion, chopped
4 tbsp lard
1 tbsp paprika
sweet green or red pepper, chopped (optional)
2 tbsp salt
¼ tsp black pepper
1 bay leaf
2 cups water
½ cup rice
1½ to 2 tbsp flour
½ pint sour cream

Brown chicken and onion in lard. Add paprika and quickly stir-fry chicken. Add green pepper and fry until lightly browned. Add salt, pepper and bay leaf. Continue cooking in covered frying pan or in oven roaster until half-done (about 20 to 30 minutes). Add water and rice and continue to cook until rice and chicken are tender. If using dumplings, omit the rice, cook chicken until tender and thicken juice by adding flour mixed with sour cream at the end of the cooking.

Dumplings
4 eggs
1½ to 2 cups all-purpose flour
½ cup water

Beat eggs. Add enough flour and water to form a medium-soft batter. Half fill a large kettle with boiling salted water. Cut (with a knife) the dough to ½ tsp size into water and put on lid. Cook 10 minutes. Drain, rinse with cool water and serve with juice from chicken.

Wine Sauce *(Bormartas)*

2 egg yolks
2 tbsp sugar
½ cup white wine
1 tbsp lemon juice

Beat egg yolks and sugar until thick and lemon-coloured. Transfer
to double boiler. Add wine and lemon juice and continue beating
over boiling water until thickened. Serve with fish, chicken or
veal.
Yield 1 cup.

Stuffed Green Peppers or Kohlrabi
(Töltött Zöldpaprika-Kalarábé)

12 green peppers or kohlrabi
1 lb ground pork
1 lb ground beef
½ cup rice
1 tsp paprika
1 tsp salt
1 egg, slightly beaten
1 onion, finely chopped
2 tbsp fat
1½ cups strained tomatoes or tomato juice

Remove stems from peppers and scoop out seeds. Avoid breaking
the shells. If using kohlrabi or combination of both, peel kohlrabi,
cut off root and scoop a large hollow out on root end. Combine
the meat, rice, paprika, salt and egg. Brown the onion in fat and
add to meat mixture. Pack loosely in the peppers or kohlrabi.
Arrange in a baking dish and pour in the tomato juice. Cook in
a moderately hot oven (375°F) for 1 to 1½ hours. The meat should
then be well-done and the peppers tender, but not broken. This
meat mixture may also be used for cabbage rolls.
Serves 6.

Transylvanian Veal Stew *(Borjútokány)*

¼ cup fat
2 lb veal, cut in 2-inch pieces
1 tsp salt
½ tsp black pepper
1 cup shredded onions

Heat fat. Add meat, salt and pepper. Cover and steam slowly until meat is nearly tender and quite dry. Stir in onions, cover and cook with the meat until both are tender and beginning to brown. If they start to brown before becoming tender, add ½ cup water. The meat should remain moist and be only lightly browned.

What gulás (goulash) is to the people of the lowlands of Hungary, tokány (stew) is to the Transylvanians. The difference lies in the use of black pepper instead of paprika.

Roast Chicken with Mushroom Stuffing
(Gombával Töltött Sütt Csirke)

5 lb roasting chicken
½ lb mushrooms, chopped
½ cup chopped celery (optional)
¼ cup butter
3 large rolls or 6 slices bread, moistened in milk
giblets, cooked and chopped
2 hard-boiled eggs, chopped
1 raw egg
2 tbsp parsley (optional)
½ tsp salt
⅛ tsp pepper

Rub chicken with salt, inside and out. Brown mushrooms and celery in butter. Combine with softened bread, giblets, cooked and raw egg, parsley, salt and pepper. Stuff chicken loosely, sew up and roast uncovered, in a slow oven (300°F) for 2½ hours or until tender. Baste chicken with drippings every half hour while roasting. If necessary, increase heat a little toward the end, to brown.
Serves 8.

Beef Steak with Mushrooms *(Gombás Rostélyos)*

3 lb round or rump steak
1 tsp salt
⅛ tsp pepper
bacon fat
2 strips bacon, chopped
2 onions, finely chopped
1 tbsp chopped parsley
1 lb mushrooms, sliced
1 cup cooked tomatoes

Sprinkle beef with salt and pepper and pound it well. Brown quickly on both sides, in bacon fat. Meanwhile, fry chopped bacon, add onions, parsley and mushrooms and brown lightly. Combine meat and mushroom mixtures, add tomatoes and simmer until sauce is thick and meat is tender.
Serves 8.

"Paprika invaded Hungary with the Turkish conquest. At first, only the peasants used it but today no Hungarian kitchen is without a liberal supply of native grown paprika—bright red and finely ground."—from *The Art of Hungarian Cooking.*

Corn Meal Mush with Cottage Cheese *(Puliszka)*

1½ cups corn meal
4 cups boiling water (or ½ milk, ½ water)
1½ tsp salt
2 cups cottage cheese
¼ cup melted butter

Gradually add corn meal to boiling water. Add salt and continue to boil gently until very thick. Pour a layer of mush about 1 inch thick into a buttered baking dish. Spread with a ½-inch-thick layer of cottage cheese and sprinkle with melted butter. Continue in layers until all the cottage cheese is used, ending with a layer of mush. Sprinkle top with butter. Bake at 375°F for 30 minutes or until slightly browned. Turn onto a warm platter to serve. Serve as dessert or at any time.
Serves 8.

Walnut Torte

1½ cups cake flour
2 tsp baking powder
¼ tsp salt
7 eggs, separated
1 cup white sugar
8 tbsp water
¾ cup ground walnuts
1 tsp vanilla

Sift together flour, baking powder and salt. Beat egg yolks with sugar until thick. Gradually add water and dry ingredients to yolk mixture and blend until smooth. Stir in walnuts and vanilla. Beat egg whites until stiff; fold in gently. Bake at 350°F for 25 to 30 minutes.
Yield three 9-inch layers.

Kifli

First Part
½ lb shortening
½ cup flour

Second Part
1 pkg dry yeast
lukewarm water
1 tsp sugar
2 cups flour
1 egg
pinch salt
sweet cream

Prepare first part by creaming shortening and beating with flour until smooth. For second part, sprinkle yeast into a little lukewarm water in which 1 tsp of sugar has been dissolved. When yeast has dissolved, mix together with flour, egg and salt. Add enough sweet cream or milk to make dough easy to roll. Roll out thinly and spread first part on top of second part. Fold together by bringing all sides to the middle. Fold in half. Refrigerate ½ hour. Roll out thinly and fold again in same manner as above. Refrigerate again. Do this three times. Roll out dough and cut into 3-inch squares. Place jam or a walnut/sugar filling in centre of each square. To shape kiflis, roll up the square starting at one corner, and bend into a crescent shape. Bake on cookie sheet at 350°F to 375°F for 15 minutes or until crisp and golden.

Dobos Torte

Batter
6 eggs
120 g sugar
150 g flour

Filling (Dobos cream)
3 egg yolks
300 g powdered sugar
70 g cocoa
350 g butter
100 to 200 g sugar cubes

Prepare the batter using 6 eggs, granulated sugar and flour. Pour into six round, very shallow baking pans which have been greased with butter and floured. Bake. Stir egg yolks into powdered sugar until completely dissolved, and then mix with cocoa and butter. Pour equal amounts of the butter cream over five of the baked layers, stack on top of one another, spread the sides and top with butter cream, and then freeze. Spread the last layer with melted sugar cubes, and cut into the desired number of slices with a slender butter knife. Freeze. When the layer is chilled, place on top of the filled torte. To serve, slice with a knife that has been dipped in hot water.

Pickled Beets *(Cékla)*

6 medium beets
½ tsp caraway seed
1 tsp salt
1 tbsp horseradish
3 tbsp sugar
½ cup vinegar
¼ cup water

Boil beets until tender; peel and slice. In a wide-mouthed jar, arrange layers of beet slices, caraway seed, salt and horseradish. Combine sugar, vinegar and water and pour over beets. Let stand in refrigerator for several hours before serving. They will be equally good after several days.
Serves 6.

India

Samosa

1½ cups flour
½ tsp salt
⅓ cup shortening
warm water
8 large potatoes
1 cup green peas
3 tbsp oil
1 tsp ground coriander
½ tsp chili powder
1 tsp cumin seed
salt, pepper and lemon juice to taste
2 cups oil for frying

Make pastry of flour, salt, shortening and enough warm water to form a hard dough. Set aside. Peel potatoes and cut into small pieces. Boil with peas until tender. Heat the 3 tbsp of oil. Add spices, potatoes, peas, salt, pepper and lemon juice mixed together. Stir-fry for a short time. Divide pastry into small balls and roll out in thin pancake rounds. Cut in half. Lift half and make into a cone, sealing it with a little water. Fill with filling and seal. Deep fry until golden brown. Serve as a snack.
Yield 24.

Pakoras

½ cup besan (chick pea flour)
¼ tsp baking soda
5 tbsp cold water
1 small onion, cut lengthwise (very thin)
½ cup finely chopped, peeled raw potato or other vegetable
⅓ tbsp chopped fresh coriander
½ tsp ground cumin
½ tsp ground hot red pepper
1 tsp salt
vegetable oil

In a deep bowl, make a smooth batter of flour, baking soda and water. Stir in onion, potato, spices and salt. In an electric pan, heat 3 cups oil until hot. Drop batter (1 tsp) into hot oil. Cook until browned. Serve as a snack with sauce (hot, plum, mango chutney).

Chappatis

2 cups whole wheat flour
2 cups white flour
1 tsp salt
3 tbsp melted butter
water

Sift together the two flours and salt. Thoroughly mix in the melted butter. Add enough water to make a soft dough. Knead well. The more you knead, the lighter it will be. Cover with a damp cloth and set aside for 1 hour. Knead thoroughly again. Form into 8 to 10 small balls and roll out into paper-thin pieces, the size of a pancake. Heat a heavy skillet or griddle. Wipe with greased paper and cook the chappatis, turning now and again until slightly browned but not hardened, 5 to 7 minutes. Wipe the skillet again after each chappati is cooked. To serve, brush with butter and eat while very hot. For puffiness, put cooked chappatis on lowest rack of a 350°F oven for a few minutes, watching carefully. Graham, barley, oatmeal or rice flour may be substituted for whole wheat.

Nan

1 pkg yeast
¼ cup warm water
1 tbsp sugar
2 tsp salt
¼ cup melted butter
¼ cup yogurt or buttermilk
1 cup lukewarm water
1 egg, beaten
2¾ to 3¼ cups white flour
melted butter
poppy seeds

Dissolve yeast in ¼ cup warm water. Combine sugar, salt, ¼ cup melted butter, yogurt and lukewarm water. Add egg and dissolved yeast. Stir in enough flour to make a soft dough. Cover and set aside for 1 hour. Knead on a floured board. Divide into even-sized balls. Let rest for 10 minutes. Meanwhile, remove racks from oven and heat to 450°F. Take one or two balls at a time and pat into oval or oblong pieces about ¼ inch thick. Brush tops with melted butter and sprinkle with a few poppy seeds. Carefully slip the nan onto the oven floor. Bake about 10 minutes or until the tops are puffy and brown. If they do not brown on the top as well as expected, slide them under the broiler for a minute or two. Serve very hot. Especially good with tandoori chicken.

In India, kalonji or nigella (black seeds similar to onion seeds) are sprinkled on the top.

Puri

1 lb whole wheat flour
4 tbsp butter or shortening
¼ cup water
½ tsp salt
oil for frying

Put 3 cups flour in bowl. Add all ingredients (except oil) using enough water to make a hard dough. Add more flour if necessary. Cut out 2 dozen pieces and form into small balls. Roll thinly. Put oil in pan for deep frying and let it get very hot. Cook one puri at a time, until light brown.

Stuffed Paratha

1 recipe chappati dough
2 tbsp butter
1 small onion, minced
¼ tsp finely chopped ginger
1 clove garlic, crushed
¼ tsp cayenne pepper
1 cup cooked mashed potato or cauliflower
½ tsp salt
melted butter

Heat 2 tbsp butter and brown onion. Add ginger, garlic and cayenne. Fry for 2 to 3 minutes. Remove from heat and mix with mashed potato and salt. Roll out dough into pancakes. Spread some filling on one paratha and cover with another, sealing edges with a little milk. Grease griddle. Brush parathas with melted butter. Fry on both sides until crisp and brown. Serve with main course or as lunch.

Meat Filling: may be made by substituting ½ lb cooked ground beef or lamb for the mashed potato.

Filling Variations:

Green Peas
1 cup cooked green peas
1 tsp chopped mint leaves
pinch turmeric
¼ tsp cumin
½ tsp salt
¼ tsp cayenne pepper
squeeze of lime juice
1 tbsp butter

Combine all ingredients and sauté in butter for 2 to 3 minutes.

Radish *(Mooli)*
1 cup grated radish
1 tsp grated ginger
½ tsp chili powder
1 tsp salt
1 tbsp butter

Squeeze excess moisture from grated radish. Mix together radish, ginger, chili powder and salt. Heat butter and cook radish mixture over low heat for 2 to 3 minutes.

Hot Breakfast

4 tbsp butter
1 cup wheatlets or cream of wheat
2 cups hot water or milk
¾ cup white sugar
4 green cardamom pods, crushed
24 blanched almonds, sliced
raisins and nuts

Melt butter in pan and add wheatlets. Fry, stirring constantly until light brown. Add water, stir until thick and add sugar, cardamom and almonds. Keep at medium heat until it thickens. Remove from heat and press into a square pan. Sprinkle with raisins and nuts. Let rest for 5 minutes and cut into 2-inch squares.

Sabzi Pilau

2 tbsp ghee (clarified butter)
2 tbsp vegetable oil
3 small onions, chopped
2 cloves garlic, minced
2 cups long grain rice
4 cups hot water
2½ tsp salt
1 tsp garam masala
3 medium carrots, cut in sticks
¼ lb green beans, sliced
½ sweet green pepper, chopped
1 medium potato, peeled and diced
¼ lb fresh peas

Heat ghee and oil together in large skillet and sauté onions until soft and golden. Add garlic and fry for 3 minutes. Add rice and sauté for 3 minutes over medium heat, stirring frequently. Stir in hot water, salt and garam masala and bring to a boil. Reduce heat to very low, cover and cook 10 minutes. Set vegetables on top of rice, cover and cook for 15 minutes or until vegetables are just cooked. Gently mix vegetables through rice and serve immediately. (Other vegetables, except squash, may be used.) *Serves 6.*

Basmati Rice

2 cups basmati rice
1 medium onion, chopped
¼ tsp salt
1 tsp cumin powder
½ tsp garam masala
3 cups boiling water

Wash rice well. In a heavy skillet, brown onion in a little oil. Add salt, cumin and garam masala. Stir. Add rice. Stir and heat for a few seconds, then add boiling water. Return to a boil, reduce heat to simmer, cover and cook 10 to 15 minutes.

Keema Mattar Pilau

2 cups long grain rice
3 tbsp oil
1¼ tsp cumin seeds
2 small onions, minced
1 clove garlic, minced
1 tsp grated fresh ginger
5 whole cloves
½ lb ground lamb, beef or chicken
½ lb shelled peas
4 cups hot water
2½ tsp salt
1 tsp garam masala

Wash, drain and dry rice. Sauté cumin seeds, onion, garlic, ginger
and cloves in oil for 5 minutes or until onions are golden. Stir
in meat and cook until browned. Add peas, water, salt and rice.
Stir well and bring to a boil. Reduce heat, cover and cook for 15
minutes. Sprinkle on garam masala, cover and cook for 10 minutes or until rice is tender.
Serves 6.

Fish and Potato Chops

1 lb cooked white fish
2 cups mashed potato
1 large onion, grated
2 tbsp chopped green pepper
fresh coriander leaves
1 tsp coriander powder
1 tsp salt
¼ tsp black pepper
¼ tsp red pepper
½ tsp garlic
1 cup chick pea flour

Mash cooked fish and potato together. Add onion, pepper, fresh and powdered coriander, salt, black and red pepper, and garlic. Form into small patties. Put flour in a bowl. Add enough water to make a thin batter. Dip patties in batter and fry in hot oil until crisp. Serve hot with sauce or chutney.

Chicken Curry

3 or 4 lb cut-up chicken
2 large onions, grated (½ lb)
1 tsp cumin seeds
½ tsp chili powder
2 tsp coriander powder
1 tsp turmeric
½ tsp black pepper
¼ tsp cloves
¼ tsp cardamom
1 tsp allspice
6 bay leaves
2 tsp salt
1 tsp garlic powder
¼ cup oil
4 red tomatoes, cut in small pieces (fresh, canned or frozen)

Mix all spices with grated onion and ¼ cup water. Put oil in pan. Add onion mixture. Stir over medium heat until brown. Add chicken and tomato and stir about 10 minutes. Add 2 cups water and continue cooking on medium heat for about an hour.

Lamb Curry

2 lb lamb, cubed
½ tsp chili powder
½ tsp black pepper
1 tsp coriander powder
1 tsp turmeric
1 tsp garlic powder or 3 whole cloves garlic
¼ tsp ground cloves
¼ tsp cardamom
4 bay leaves
2 large onions, grated
2 tbsp oil
2 large red tomatoes
1 cup water

Mix all spices and onion together into oil and fry until brown. Add lamb, tomato and water. Cook 1 hour or until lamb is tender.

Tandoori Chicken

2 lb chicken
½ tsp saffron
1½ tbsp boiling water
3 cloves garlic
1½ tbsp grated fresh ginger
2 tbsp lemon juice
¼ tsp chili powder
1½ tsp paprika
1 tsp garam masala
1½ tsp salt
2 tbsp vegetable oil

Remove skin from chicken and prick flesh with knife to allow spices to penetrate. Mix saffron with boiling water. Purée garlic, ginger and lemon juice in blender. Pour into small bowl and add chili powder, paprika, garam masala, salt and saffron. Spread over chicken and rub in well. Refrigerate, marinating for 7 hours or overnight. Put oil in baking dish and add chicken. Baste chicken with oil and roast in 400°F oven, breast down, for 30 minutes. Turn over, baste again and cook for 1 minutes. Baste with pan juices every 5 minutes until chicken is cooked. (Do not overcook.)
Serves 4.

Lamb Korma

Masala
¼ cup raw cashews
3 dried hot red chilies, stemmed and seeded
1-inch piece fresh ginger root, scraped and quartered
2-inch piece stick cinnamon, crushed
¼ tsp cardamom seeds
3 whole cloves
2 large cloves garlic, peeled
2 tbsp white poppy seeds
1 tbsp coriander seeds
1 tsp cumin seeds

Combine nuts, chilies, ginger and 1 cup cold water in blender. Blend at high speed for 1 minute or until the mixture is reduced to a smooth purée. Scrape down sides. Add all other ingredients and blend again, until completely pulverized. Set aside.

Lamb
½ tsp saffron threads
6 tbsp ghee (clarified butter)
1 cup finely chopped onions
2 tsp salt
½ cup plain yogurt
1½ lb lean boneless lamb, cut in 2-inch cubes
2 tbsp fresh coriander, finely chopped
1 tbsp fresh lemon juice

Place saffron in small bowl and cover with ¼ cup boiling water. Let soak 10 minutes. Meanwhile, in a heavy skillet heat ghee over medium heat until a drop of water splutters when flicked into it. Add onions and fry, stirring constantly until soft and golden (7 to 8 minutes). Stir in the salt and masala, then add the yogurt. Cook over moderate heat, stirring occasionally, until ghee lightly films the surface. Add lamb, stirring to coat pieces evenly. Squeeze the saffron and add it and soaking liquid to skillet. Reduce heat to low, cover tightly and cook for 20 minutes, turning lamb occasionally. Scatter 1 tbsp of fresh coriander over the meat and continue cooking tightly covered for 10 minutes more or until lamb is tender.

To serve, transfer the entire contents of the skillet to a heated platter, sprinkle the top with lemon juice and remaining fresh coriander.

Gulab Jaman

2 cups instant powdered milk
½ cup white flour
½ tsp baking soda
¼ cup butter
¼ cup milk
oil for frying
3 cups sugar
2 cups water
12 cardamom seeds, crushed

Mix together milk powder, flour, soda and butter. Add enough milk to make a firm dough. Shape into 1-inch balls. Heat oil and deep fry six to eight balls at a time, turning with slotted spoon. Remove when browned. Soak in syrup for about two hours before serving.

Syrup: Combine sugar and water. Bring to a boil over moderate heat. Boil, stirring constantly until sugar is dissolved. Increase heat to high and cook undisturbed for 5 minutes. Add cardamom and set aside over very low heat, until ready to use.

Nut and Sesame Ladoo

1 cup toasted sesame seeds
¾ cup peanuts
1 cup cashews
2 tbsp ghee (clarified butter)
½ cup firmly packed brown sugar
½ cup white sugar
½ cup water
pinch salt

Grind toasted sesame seeds to a paste in electric blender. Fry peanuts and cashews in ghee, until golden brown. Cool and chop finely. Mix with ground sesame seeds and set aside. Combine sugars and water. Bring to a boil and cook until it reaches the soft ball stage (234°F on candy thermometer). Stir the nut-sesame mixture into the syrup. Add salt and mix thoroughly. Grease hands and shape into balls the size of walnuts.

Noodle Pudding *(Simay)*

½ cup thin spaghetti noodles
1 tbsp butter
½ cup water
1 litre whole milk
¼ cup white sugar
5 green cardamoms, crushed
2 tbsp golden raisins
20 almonds

Break noodles into ½-inch lengths. Fry them in butter until lightly browned. Add water and cook over low heat, in a covered pan. After the water has gone, add the milk. Cook 1 hour over low heat, until the pudding thickens. Soak almonds in water, peel and chop finely. Add sugar, crushed cardamom, raisins and almonds.

Almond and Pistachio Candy
(Badam Pistaz Burfi)

4 tsp ghee (clarified butter)
1 quart milk
1 cup sugar
1 cup ground almonds or 1 cup slivered, blanched almonds, pulverized
1 cup unsalted pistachios, pulverized
½ tsp almond extract

With a pastry brush, spread 1 tsp of the ghee on a 7½-inch pie plate. In a heavy 3- to 4-quart saucepan, bring milk to a boil over high heat. Reduce heat to moderate and, stirring frequently, cook for about 35 minutes or until milk thickens to the consistency of heavy cream. Add sugar and stir for 10 minutes longer. Still stirring, add 3 tsp of the ghee and cook for another 5 to 10 minutes, until the mixture is thick enough to draw away from the sides of the pan in a solid mass. Remove pan from heat and stir in the almond extract. Pour candy into the pie plate, spreading and smoothing it with a spatula. Let cool for 30 minutes or so, then cut it into about 24 small squares or diamonds. It will harden to the consistency of fudge as it cools.

Jallebis

1 pkg yeast
¼ cup warm water
3 cups flour
water
¼ tsp saffron or yellow colouring
3 cups sugar
2 cups water
vegetable oil for frying*

Dissolve yeast in ¼ cup warm water. Combine flour, dissolved yeast and enough water to make a smooth, pancake-like batter. Add saffron and beat for several minutes. Set aside for 30 minutes. Meanwhile, combine sugar and 2 cups water; boil to make a syrup about the consistency of corn syrup. Keep warm while waiting for use. Heat the vegetable oil in a heavy pan to about 365°F, for deep frying. Put some of the batter in a funnel (keep your finger over the spout). Using finger to control the amount of batter, move the funnel in concentric circles over the hot fat. Cook on each side until golden and crisp. Remove and drain. Dip each jallebi in the warm syrup for a minute or two. Drain again. Plan to eat them soon after they are made since they will not keep the proper crispness for long.
*For a richer flavour, half vegetable oil and half clarified butter may be used for deep frying if desired.

In India, a coconut shell with one hole is used instead of the funnel. A plastic ketchup or mustard dispenser may be used.

Ireland

Green Pea Soup

½ lb green split peas
1½ pints stock or water
2 medium onions
2 oz fat
1 large carrot
1 large potato
2 celery stalks
a few bacon pieces
salt and pepper

Wash split peas and soak overnight in ½ pint cold water. Use this water in the soup. Chop onions. Heat fat in heavy pan or pressure cooker; add onions and fry them gently until soft, about 10 minutes. Chop or grate vegetables and add to onions with bacon, soaked peas and all the liquid. Season with pepper only. Cover and simmer for 1 to 1½ hours (20 minutes in pressure cooker). This soup is even better if passed through a sieve or blender. Salt to taste. Serve hot with croutons or toast. Soup can be reheated.

Leek and Potato Soup

1 lb potatoes
1 large onion
1 lb leeks
2 oz butter
2 pints water
½ pint milk
salt and pepper, to taste

Peel and chop potatoes roughly. Slice onion. Wash leeks well and slice. Heat butter in a heavy pan and add leeks, onions and potatoes. Cover and cook gently, 15 to 20 minutes, stirring occasionally. Be careful not to brown the vegetables. Add water and seasonings, bring to boil, reduce heat and simmer 20 minutes. Pass through a sieve or blend until smooth. Return to pan, add milk and heat thoroughly. Serve sprinkled with chopped chives or parsley.

Whole Wheat Bannock

¼ cup bran
1 cup whole wheat flour
1 cup all-purpose flour
1 cup rolled oats
3 heaping tsp powdered buttermilk
1 heaping tsp baking soda
½ tsp salt
1½ cups cold water
⅓ cup blackstrap molasses

Mix together dry ingredients. Add water and molasses. Mix to form a soft dough. Knead and shape into a circle the size of a dinner plate. Place on greased and floured cookie sheet. Bake at 375°F for 40 to 50 minutes.

Irish Soda Bread

2 cups flour
1 tbsp sugar
1½ tsp baking powder
1 tsp baking soda
¼ tsp salt
¼ cup butter or margarine, softened
¾ cup raisins
1½ tsp caraway seed (optional)
1 cup buttermilk
1 egg, slightly beaten with 1 tbsp water

Sift flour, sugar, baking powder, soda and salt into large mixing bowl. Cut in butter with a pastry blender until mixture resembles coarse meal. Stir in raisins and caraway. Add buttermilk, blending to moisten the dry ingredients. Turn dough onto floured board and knead for several minutes until smooth. Form dough into a round ball and place on greased baking sheet. Flatten until dough is about 1½ inches high; brush top and sides with beaten egg mixture. Cut a ½-inch deep cross in top of bread with sharp knife. Bake at 375°F for 30 to 40 minutes or until a wooden pick, inserted in the centre, comes out clean. Cool on a wire rack. Brush top with butter or margarine and cover with cloth.
Makes 1 loaf.

Fadge (Potato Bread)

1 cup mashed potatoes
1 tbsp margarine
½ cup all-purpose flour
¼ tsp salt

Mix together all ingredients. Knead well. Roll dough on a floured board until thin. Prick with a fork. Cut into 4 pieces. Cook quickly in a lightly greased frying pan or griddle. Serve hot with butter.

Seafood and Mushroom Pie

1 lb potatoes
seafood of your choice (e.g., 4 cups mussels in the shell or
   8 large scallops)
1½ oz butter
1½ oz flour
1 cup milk
6 oz sliced mushrooms
1 tbsp chopped parsley
4 tbsp sherry
salt and pepper

Boil potatoes and mash with butter and milk. Set aside. Scrub
shellfish very well. Place in salted water and bring to a boil.
Cook until shells open. Cool and remove fish from shells. Melt
butter, stir in flour and add milk to make a thick sauce. Add
mushrooms, fish, parsley and sherry. Season to taste. Place in
an ovenproof dish, cover with mashed potatoes and bake at
350°F until lightly browned (20 to 30 minutes).

Oyster Soufflé

1 dozen oysters, shelled and chopped
juice of 1 lemon
3 oz fresh bread crumbs
8 oz whipping cream
3 eggs, separated
pinch nutmeg
salt and pepper

Preheat oven to 350°F. Grease four individual soufflé dishes or
one 6-inch dish. Save liquid from oysters, add to lemon juice
and heat to warm. Place bread crumbs in a large bowl and add
liquid. Add cream, beaten egg yolks, oysters and seasoning. Let
stand ½ hour, or until ready to bake. Beat egg whites until stiff
and fold into mixture. Pour into preheated dish (dishes). Bake
30 minutes for individual dishes or 40 to 45 minutes for large
dish. Serve as soon as it is well-risen and lightly browned.

Minted Mayo Lamb

2 to 3 potatoes per person
4 to 5 lb lamb leg or shoulder
salt
1 large onion, sliced
3 to 4 sprigs mint
2 tbsp vegetable oil
chopped parsley and chives

Heat oven to 325°F. Scrub or peel potatoes. Rub lamb well with salt, place in roasting pan and arrange potatoes around the meat. Scatter onion and mint over meat and pour on the oil. Cover and roast for 2 hours, basting from time to time. When meat seems well done, remove the cover and the mint. Return meat to oven (raising temperature to 375°F if necessary) to brown. When the top is crisp, remove to a serving dish. Place potatoes in a separate dish, garnish with parsley and chives and keep hot. Make gravy with the juices in the pan. Serve with a green vegetable.

Irish Stew

2 lb end neck of lamb or neck chops
salt and pepper
1 lb onions
4 celery stalks
1 leek
½ lb carrots
1½ lb potatoes
2 oz barley
¾ pint cold water
chopped fresh parsley

Ask the butcher to cut a whole neck of lamb into circles or use neck chops. Season meat well. Slice onions thinly, other vegetables thickly and wash the barley. Pack alternate layers of vegetables, barley and meat in an ovenproof casserole, starting with onions and covering the top with potatoes. Pour water over all, cover and place in preheated oven (325°F). Cook for 1½ to 2 hours, basting potatoes with liquid occasionally. When the meat is just tender, raise oven temperature to 425°F and continue to cook for 15 to 20 minutes to brown the potatoes. Garnish with chopped parsley.

Honey Oat Crunch

4 oz butter or margarine
1 rounded tbsp honey
3 oz soft brown sugar
4 oz self-rising flour
pinch salt
2 tsp ground ginger
4 oz porridge oats

Grease two large baking sheets. Melt butter and honey together. Mix together all other ingredients and add melted mixture. Stir well—it should be firm. Form into small balls (tsp), place on baking sheet and flatten slightly. Bake at 350°F for 15 minutes or until golden. Cool on sheet for a few minutes then remove to a wire rack. Store in airtight tin.

Inver Fruit Loaf

1 lb mixed dried fruit
½ pint hot, strong tea
1½ lb self-rising flour
pinch salt
2 tsp mixed spice
1 tsp ground ginger
½ lb brown sugar
½ lb butter or margarine
2 eggs
milk, as required

Soak fruit in tea overnight. Grease two 2-lb loaf tins. Sift flour, salt and spices into a large bowl. Add sugar. Rub in butter. Beat eggs and add to flour along with fruit. Stir well. Add milk if necessary to make dough a heavy dropping consistency. Divide between tins. Bake at 350°F for 45 minutes, or until firm on top. Lower heat to 325°F and bake a further 45 minutes. Cool loaves in tin for 5 minutes, turn onto a rack and wrap in foil when cold.

Sunset Pears

¼ pint water
8 oz granulated sugar
½ lemon
8 cooking pears
8 whole cloves
few drops pink colouring
2 tbsp Irish whiskey

Dissolve sugar in water in a pan just large enough to hold the pears, whole, standing stalk upwards if possible. Bring syrup toa boil and add sliced lemon. Peel pears, leaving whole with stalks on. Stick a clove in each pear. Place pears upright in the pan, cover and simmer gently until tender. Carefully lift pears and place them in a glass bowl, standing upright. Remove cloves. Add enough colouring to syrup to yield a soft pink colour. Remove lemon slices and stir in whiskey. Pour syrup over pears. Chill. Serve with thick cream.

Whiskey Cream

8 oz whipping cream
1 tsp sugar
2 tbsp Irish whiskey

Whip cream until just thick. Add sugar and fold in whiskey. Chill.

Connemara Apple Cake

Base
6 oz cake flour
3 tsp baking soda
pinch salt
3 oz sugar
1 large egg
1½ oz butter
¼ pint milk

Topping
2 large baking apples
3 oz sugar
1 tsp cinnamon
1 oz butter

To prepare base, sift flour and soda together with a pinch of salt.
Add sugar. Melt butter and mix with milk and beaten egg. Stir
into dry ingredients. Beat until smooth. Pour into greased, 8-inch
round cake tin. Topping: peel, core and slice apples thinly. Cover
cake base with overlapping slices. Melt butter, brush over apple
slices, then sprinkle with a mixture of sugar and cinnamon. Place
on baking sheet and bake in the centre of the oven at 400°F for
40 to 50 minutes, or until apples are soft and cake is cooked.
Can be served warm as a pudding or cold with whipped cream.

Whiskey Punch

juice of 2 lemons
6 rounded tsp brown sugar
10 oz boiling water
5 oz Irish whiskey

Warm a jug. Put lemon juice and sugar in jug and pour in boiling
water. Stir until sugar is dissolved. Add whiskey and stir. Serve
in warm glasses.

Mint Jelly

3 lb cooking apples
1 pint water
4 tbsp vinegar
1 lb sugar for each pint apple purée
6 to 8 sprigs mint
green food colouring (optional)

Wash and quarter unpeeled apples and cook with the water until soft. Add vinegar and cook 5 minutes longer. Strain juice and measure. Return to clean pan, add sugar as required, place over low heat and stir until sugar is dissolved. Bring slowly to a boil, then boil rapidly until jelly sets. Add chopped mint and food colouring. Pour into hot, sterilized jars; seal, label and store in a dark place.

Jewish

Passover Mondlen for Soup

6 tbsp water
½ tsp salt
pinch pepper
¼ cup oil
1 cup matzo meal
2 eggs

Bring to a boil water, salt, pepper and oil. Add the matzo meal, cook and stir over a low heat until mixture forms a ball and leaves the sides of the saucepan. Remove from heat. Allow to cool a little. Beat in eggs one at a time, until dough is smooth. Oil hands lightly and shape dough into balls. Place on a well-greased cookie sheet. Bake at 400°F until golden brown.
Makes about 50.

Matzo Ball Soup *(Chicken Soup with Matzo Balls)*

Soup
1 whole or cut-up chicken
1 stalk celery
1 carrot
1 onion
salt and pepper to taste

Place chicken in large soup pot and cover with water. Add chopped celery, carrot, onion, salt and pepper. Bring to a boil and let simmer for two hours or until meat falls off the bones. Strain meat from soup. Cool soup and meat in the refrigerator overnight. Strain soup and add chicken pieces.

Matzo Balls
2 tbsp fat or oil
2 eggs, slightly beaten
½ cup matzo meal
1 tsp salt
2 tbsp chicken stock or water

Mix fat and eggs. Add matzo meal and salt. Mix well. Add soup stock or water. Cover and refrigerate 20 minutes. In a 2- or 3-quart pot, bring salted water to a boil. One at a time, form balls the size of a golf ball and drop into barely bubbling water. Cover and cook 30 to 40 minutes. Add cooked matzo balls to room temperature soup and heat soup to desired serving temperature.

Matzo Meal Latkes

3 eggs
½ cup matzo meal
dash of cinnamon
¾ cup water
½ tsp sugar
½ tsp salt

Separate egg whites from yolks. Beat egg whites until stiff. Add all ingredients to the beaten yolks, folding in the beaten whites last. Drop by the spoonful onto a well-greased griddle and brown on both sides. Serve hot.

Noodle Kugel

8 oz pkg flat, broad noodles
2 eggs
pinch salt

Cook noodles according to package directions and drain well. Beat eggs. Add eggs and salt to noodles. Mix well. Place in greased baking pan. Bake at 375°F, until nicely brown on top. If desired, a little apricot jam may be dotted on top before baking.

Carrot Tzimmes

2 lb carrots, sliced
1 egg
½ cup liquid honey
⅓ cup brown sugar
⅓ cup chicken fat (or oil)
½ cup flour
½ cup raisins or prunes

Boil carrots for 3 to 4 minutes. Mix egg, honey, sugar and fat. Blend in flour. Add parboiled carrots. Add raisins or prunes. Bake in well-greased pan at 350°F for 1 hour.

Potato Kugel

5 large potatoes
1 onion, grated
3 eggs
⅓ cup matzo meal
½ cup melted fat
1 tsp salt
¼ tsp pepper
¼ tsp cinnamon (optional)

Grate potatoes on a fine grater; drain off most of the water. Add grated onion, eggs and other ingredients. Mix well. Pour into well-greased heated pudding dish and bake in a hot oven (400°F) for about 1 hour or until a brown crust has formed on top.
Note: To make the kugel lighter in texture and colour, substitute one large mashed potato for one of the raw potatoes, and decrease the matzo meal to ½ cup.
Serves 6 to 8.

Passover Chopped Chicken Balls

3 large onions
breast of raw chicken
3 eggs
½ glass cold water
1 tbsp salt
1 tsp pepper
1 tsp sugar
½ cup matzo meal
2 carrots

Chop two onions, chicken and eggs together, adding water gradually. Add salt, pepper, sugar and matzo meal. Chop very finely. Form into balls and drop into boiling water. Slice remaining onion and carrots and add to water, seasoning to taste. Cook for 2½ hours.

Cabbage Rolls

1 cabbage
2 onions
1 lb ground beef
½ cup uncooked rice
salt and pepper
1 large can tomatoes
1 can cream of tomato soup
1 slice lemon
raisins

Boil cabbage whole, removing leaves as they soften. Set leaves aside. Chop 1 onion; combine with beef and rice and season to taste. Divide mixture into enough equal-sized portions for the number of cabbage leaves. Place mixture on centre of leaves, fold sides over filling and roll up. Combine tomatoes, soup, 1 sliced onion, lemon slice and some raisins (as many or few as you like), in a large pot. Bring to a boil, add cabbage rolls and simmer for 2 hours. Before serving, place in ovenproof dish and bake at 350°F for ½ hour.

Passover Komish

3 eggs
¾ cup sugar
¾ cup oil
2 tbsp potato starch
¾ cup almonds or crushed walnuts
½ tsp salt
1 tsp cinnamon
¾ cup matzo cake meal (approximately)
¼ cup matzo meal
cinnamon/sugar

Beat eggs, sugar and oil. Add dry ingredients (except cinnamon/sugar), mix well, then set in refrigerator for about ½ hour. Moisten hands with oil and shape mixture into four rolls or long rectangles. (If mixture is too soft to handle, add more cake meal.) Bake at 350°F about 20 to 30 minutes. Cool rolls about 10 minutes. Cut into slices. Dredge slices in cinnamon/sugar and place back on flat pan. Dry in 200°F oven until light brown and crisp, about ½ hour.

Ginger Squares *(Ingberlach)*

1 lb (16 oz) honey
1 cup sugar
3 cups matzo farfel
¼ tsp powdered ginger
½ cup chopped nuts

Combine honey and sugar. Heat and stir in saucepan over low heat until mixture comes to a boil. Combine matzo farfel and ginger, blending well; add slowly to honey mixture, continuing to cook until syrup is brown and thick. Moisten a pastry board; spread honey mixture over board. Sprinkle nuts over top. Chill. When firm, cut into squares.

Cheese Blintzes

4 eggs
1½ cups white flour
3 cups water
salt to taste

Beat eggs. Add flour, water and salt. Beat until smooth. Heat and lightly grease pan. Pour ¼ cup of batter into pan for each pancake. Cook one side and turn out onto a towel, fried side up. On each, spread some filling, roll up and fry in butter until brown.

Filling
½ lb cottage cheese
1 egg yolk (or 1 whole egg)
salt, sugar and cinnamon to taste

Blend well. Use approximately 1 tbsp filling for each blintze.

Lebanon

Lentil Soup

1 cup lentils
4 cups water
2 onions, chopped finely
¼ cup olive oil
1 clove garlic, crushed
2 cups chopped spinach
juice of 1 lemon (optional)
salt and pepper, to taste

Rinse and drain lentils. Put lentils and water into soup pot and boil until tender, about 25 minutes. Fry onions in oil and garlic until brown. Add spinach to lentils. Add onions and remaining ingredients to soup. Cook for 20 minutes longer. Serve hot.

Kishk Soup *(Shourabit Kishk)*

½ cup beef or lamb, finely diced
1 small onion, finely chopped
2 cloves garlic, finely chopped
1 cup kishk
4 to 5 cups water
salt to taste

Sauté meat, onion and garlic over medium heat, until onion is transparent. Stir in kishk and water. Bring to a boil over medium heat, stirring occasionally. Add salt, lower heat and simmer for 10 to 15 minutes. Add more water if necessary. Serve with pita bread. (Kishk is available at specialty food stores.)

Eggplant Dip

1 large eggplant
1 to 2 tbsp tahini (sesame butter)
salt to taste
1 clove garlic
¼ cup lemon juice

Bake eggplant at 350°F until soft. Peel and chop. Add remaining ingredients and blend well in food processor or blender. Serve with pita bread and raw vegetables.

Hummus with Tahini

1 can chick peas (19 oz)
1 to 2 tbsp tahini (sesame butter)
1 clove garlic, crushed
½ tsp salt
¼ cup lemon juice
water

Mash chick peas in food processor or blender. Blend together crushed garlic, tahini, salt and lemon juice. Add to processed chick peas. Thin with a little cold water if desired.

Yogurt *(Laban)*

2 quarts whole milk
2 tbsp yogurt starter (rawbi)*

Place milk in a heavy, non-aluminium pan. Bring to a boil over medium heat, being careful not to scorch it. Remove from heat and cool until lukewarm.** Place yogurt starter in a cup and add 4 tbsp of warm milk. Stir well and add to warmed milk. Cover pot and wrap in a blanket. Let rest, undisturbed, for 5 to 6 hours or until set. Cool in refrigerator.

*Starter may be saved from the last batch or commercial yogurt may be used.

**Milk is ready as soon as you can hold your little finger in it for a count of ten.

Avocado with Tahini

1 large ripe avocado
1 small clove garlic, crushed
juice of 1 lemon
salt to taste
2 tbsp tahini (sesame butter)

Peel and mash avocado thoroughly. Blend together crushed garlic, lemon juice, salt and tahini. Mix with avocado. Serve with crackers, pita bread or raw vegetables.

Pita Bread

1 to 2 cakes yeast
¼ cup lukewarm water
2 tbsp sugar
13 cups flour
2 tsp salt
4 cups lukewarm water
½ cup oil

Dissolve yeast in ¼ cup lukewarm water. Add sugar. Sift flour and salt together. Add water, oil and yeast mixture. Knead until dough comes away from the sides of the pan. Cover and set aside until doubled. Shape dough into balls and place on a flour-covered cloth. Cover with a dry cloth and let rest for about an hour. Roll out dough to approximately ¼-inch thickness. Allow to rest covered, for about an hour or more. Gently place each loaf on a heavy baking pan. Bake at 450° to 500°F for 7 to 10 minutes or until lightly browned on top and bottom.

Lentils and Wheat *(Imjadara)*

2 cups brown lentils
7 cups cold water
1 tbsp salt
¼ to ½ cup olive oil
1 Spanish onion
1 cup medium crushed wheat

Wash lentils well. Add water and salt. Bring to a boil and cook until tender, about 20 minutes. Meanwhile, heat oil in skillet. Slice onion in long strips and fry in oil until very brown. Pour off oil into lentils, keeping onions in pan. Add some water to pan, mashing onions. Add to lentils. Stir in wheat. Continue to cook until wheat is tender and mixture thick. (By adding more water, mixture will be thinner and may be served as soup.) May be served hot or cold. With pita bread and a salad, this is a complete dinner. A little lemon juice may be drizzled over each serving.

Okra

2 lb okra
¼ cup olive oil
1 medium onion, finely chopped
2 cloves garlic, finely chopped
1½ tsp coriander
salt and pepper
1 cup tomato sauce or juice
2 cups water

Heat oil in pot. Sauté onion until transparent. Add remaining ingredients. Bring to a boil, reduce heat to low and cook until okra is tender about 30 minutes.

Cucumber and Yogurt Salad

1 clove garlic
1 tsp salt
2 cups yogurt
1 English cucumber
1 tbsp chopped fresh mint

Crush garlic and salt in salad bowl. Stir in yogurt. Wash cucumber. Cut lengthwise and then crosswise into thin slices. Add to yogurt and stir gently, until all slices are separated and coated. Sprinkle with mint.

Tabouli

½ cup fine cracked wheat
1 bunch green onions
2 bunches fresh parsley
fresh or dried mint, to taste
4 large tomatoes
juice of 4 lemons
½ cup olive oil
salt and pepper, to taste

Soak wheat in warm water for a few minutes. Squeeze dry. Finely chop onions, parsley, mint and tomatoes. Add wheat, lemon juice, oil, salt and pepper. Mix well. Serve with fresh lettuce, grape or cabbage leaves as scoops.
Serves 6.

Fish with Garlic Sauce *(Samak mah Tume)*

2 lb smelts
2 tsp salt
½ tsp pepper
1 cup flour
½ cup vegetable oil
3 tbsp butter
3 cloves garlic, crushed
4 tbsp lemon juice

Clean smelts and remove heads. Wash well. Add salt and pepper to flour. Dredge smelts. Heat oil in skillet and fry smelts until golden. Drain and place on a serving platter. Heat butter. Add garlic and fry until golden. Stir in lemon juice. Pour sauce over smelts.

Fried Fish *(Samak Makli)*

2 whole, white fish (4 lb)
salt
flour
1 cup oil
1 lemon
parsley

Clean fish and wash well. Sprinkle with salt, inside and out. Cut into serving-sized pieces. Place in a covered dish and refrigerate until cold, approximately 1 hour. Remove from refrigerator 15 minutes before cooking. Dredge lightly with flour. Heat oil and add fish. Turn, half-way through cooking. Garnish with lemon and parsley.

Sesame Sauce

½ cup tahini (sesame butter)
1 clove garlic
½ tsp salt
½ cup water
½ cup lemon juice

Place all ingredients in blender and process until smooth. Serve with fish.

Raw Kibbee

1 cup medium crushed wheat
1 lb ground beef or lamb
1 medium onion
1 tbsp salt
½ tsp pepper
¼ tsp ground allspice
¼ tsp ground cloves
pinch cinnamon

Soak wheat in warm water for 15 minutes. Drain. Grind meat and onion together. Add wheat, salt, pepper and spices. Mix thoroughly. Shape onto oval platter, make diamond-shaped designs on top and garnish with onion slices, radishes and parsley.

Baked Kibbee

raw kibbee (as above)
1 cup lean ground beef
1 small onion, chopped
cinnamon, allspice
butter or oil

Prepare raw kibbee as above. Set aside. Fry 1 cup beef and onion until meat is cooked. Add ¼ tsp salt and a pinch each of cinnamon and allspice. Divide raw kibbee in half. Grease a 9 x 9-inch baking pan. Spread half of raw mixture in bottom of pan. Cover with cooked meat mixture and spread balance of raw kibbee over the top. Score top in diamond shapes and spread with butter or oil. Bake at 350°F until cooked through, 30 to 60 minutes.

Cabbage Rolls *(Yabrak Malfoof)*

1 head new cabbage (3 lb)
1 cup rice
1 lb coarsely ground lamb
pepper, cinnamon & allspice, to taste
1 can tomato sauce* (14 oz)
1 can tomatoes* (28 oz)
1 tbsp salt

Core cabbage and plunge into boiling, salted water. Loosen leaves with a fork. Cook until slightly tender. Mix together rice, lamb and spices. Place approximately 1 tbsp meat mixture on inner side of each leaf. Spread across leaf in a line. Roll up. Line bottom of pan with three or four unfilled leaves. Place rolls evenly in rows, layering the rows in a crisscross manner. Use an inverted plate to hold the rolls down. Add tomato sauce, tomatoes, salt, pepper and enough water to cover rolls. Cover with a lid, bring to a boil, reduce heat to low and cook until done, about 1 hour.

*Tomato juice or fresh tomatoes may be substituted.

Variations: The same mixture may be used to stuff summer squash, small eggplants, green tomatoes or green pepper. Cover with tomato sauce, tomatoes and water and cook as above.

Grape Leaf Rolls

grape leaves
1 cup rice
1½ lb ground lamb
pepper, cinnamon, allspice, to taste
2 lemons
1 tbsp salt

Wash leaves and cover with boiling water to soften. Mix together rice, meat, spices and the juice of 1 lemon. Place 1 tbsp of meat mixture on the veined side of each leaf. Spread across leaf and roll up, turning in the sides. Line bottom of pot with a few unfilled leaves. Place rolls evenly in rows, layering rows in a crisscross manner. Use an inverted plate to hold down the rolls. Cover with water. Add salt. Bring to a boil, reduce heat to low and cook until done, about 1 hour. Serve with yogurt and lemon wedges.

Nammoura

Syrup:
1½ cups sugar
1 cup water
1 tsp lemon juice
1 tbsp flower water

Bring sugar and water to a boil over high heat. Add lemon juice and simmer for 20 minutes. Remove from heat and add flower water. Set aside.

4 cups cream of wheat
2 cups sugar
½ cup unsalted butter, softened
1 tsp baking powder
1 tsp vanilla
2 cups warm milk
8 oz almonds

In a large bowl, combine all ingredients except milk and almonds. Add enough milk to soften the mixture until it is the consistency of yogurt. Pour into greased baking dish. Bake at 350°F for 10 minutes. Remove from oven and cut into rectangular or diamond shapes. Place an almond on each piece and return to oven. Bake until golden brown, 30 to 40 minutes. Pour syrup over hot nammoura. Cool and serve.

jw

Baklawa

2 cups walnuts
½ cup sugar
1 lb unsalted butter
1 lb filo pastry
syrup (see below)

Combine nuts and sugar. Mix well and set aside. Butter a 14 x 10-inch baking pan. Melt butter. Layer filo in pan using two sheets filo; brush with melted butter, cover with two more sheets and repeat until ½ lb of filo is used (keep unused sheets covered with a damp cloth). Spread nut mixture over last layer. Top nuts with filo, using same procedure as for bottom. Bake at 350°F for 1 hour, until golden. Remove from oven and saturate with cold syrup.

Syrup
3 cups honey
1 cup water
2 tbsp lemon juice
½ tsp rose water

Combine honey and water. Stir until dissolved. Bring to a boil over medium heat and cook for 5 minutes. Add juice and rose water. Continue to boil for an additional 5 minutes. Cool.

Sesame Cookies

1 cup butter
1 cup sugar
4 eggs
peel of 1 lemon, grated
peel of 1 orange, grated
1 cup orange juice
5 cups flour
1 tsp yensoon
1 tsp mahlab
4 tsp baking powder
sesame seeds

Cream butter. Add sugar, eggs and lemon and orange peel. Beat well. Sift together flour, spices and baking powder. Add to creamed mixture alternately with juice, beating well after each addition. Break off pieces of dough and roll between your hands to form a finger shape. Fold in half, forming a loop. Wrap straight pieces around one another twice (pretzel shape). Brush with beaten egg, and roll in sesame seeds. Bake at 350°F until very lightly browned, 15 to 20 minutes.

Arabic Coffee *(Quahwa Arabia)*

1 cup cold water
1 cardamom seed
1 tsp sugar
2 tbsp Arabic coffee

Place water in small coffee pot. Crack cardamom and add to water. Bring to a boil, remove from heat and add coffee and sugar. Return to a boil and remove from heat as it foams, stirring each time; repeat this three times. Let settle. Pour into tiny cups and serve.

Mexico

The Goddess of Corn

Eggs, Ranch-Style *(Huevos Rancheros)*

2 eggs
2 corn tortillas*
Mexican sauce**
1 slice cooked ham
oil for frying

Pour oil, ¼ inch deep, into medium skillet. Heat to 365°F. Fry tortillas until crisp and lightly browned. Drain on paper towels and keep warm. In a separate pan, fry 2 eggs, sunny side up. Heat sauce and ham. Place tortillas on plate; top with ham and eggs and pour the sauce over all. May be served with refried black beans and garnished with grated cheese. It makes a hearty breakfast.
*See recipe for tortillas under "Bread."

**Mexican Sauce
1 tsp vegetable oil
½ medium onion, minced
1 large clove garlic, minced
salt
1 hot green pepper or chili pepper
1 medium can tomatoes
1 chicken bouillon cube
¼ cup hot water

Heat oil in saucepan. Sauté onion, garlic, salt and pepper. Add tomatoes (with their juice) and mash. Dilute bouillon cube in water and add to tomato mixture. Bring to a boil, stirring occasionally. Let stand for a few minutes to thicken. Serve hot.

Corn Tortillas *(Tortillas de Maiz)*

1 cup masa harina (corn flour)
½ cup warm water

Place corn flour in a medium bowl. Work in water with your fingers to make a soft dough. If dough is crumbly or dry, mix in a little more water. Shape into a ball. Cover with damp towel; let stand 20 minutes. Preheat ungreased griddle, "comal" or heavy skillet over medium heat. Line bottom of tortilla press or flat surface with plastic wrap. Divide dough into small pieces, according to the number and size of tortillas desired. Shape each piece of dough into a ball and place on lined tortilla press or flat surface. Cover with another piece of plastic wrap. Press with the palm of your hand to flatten ball slightly. Close tortilla press firmly and then open; or flatten dough by pressing with the bottom of a small, heavy skillet. If necessary, press with fingers to flatten further. Peel plastic carefully from top and bottom of tortilla. If tortilla sticks, dough is too wet; add more masa, a little at a time. If it crumbles, dough is too dry; add more water, a little at a time. Cook in preheated pan until lightly spotted with brown on each side; turn once. Stack cooked tortillas and cover with a dry cloth until ready for use. Tortillas may feel stiff as they come from the pan but will soften as they stand.
Yield 6 6-inch tortillas.

White Rice with Fried Plantain

Rice
1½ tbsp vegetable oil or butter
½ medium onion, finely sliced
1 medium clove garlic, crushed
1 tsp salt
dash pepper
1 cup converted rice
2 cups chicken broth (very hot)

Heat oil in large pot or Dutch oven. Add onion, garlic, salt and
pepper and sauté until browned. Add rice and fry until golden.
Add broth, cover and bring to a boil. After 10 minutes reduce
heat and cook until rice is tender and broth absorbed.

Plantain
2 tbsp butter
1 plantain, sliced
¼ cup white sugar
dash cinnamon

Heat butter in saucepan. Add plantain and fry until golden.
Drain on paper towel. Add sugar and cinnamon and serve over
white rice.

Red Snapper Veracruz Style
(Pescado blanco de la Veracruzana)

6 red snapper fillets (8 to 10 oz each)
¼ tsp salt
⅛ tsp pepper
⅓ cup all-purpose flour
¼ cup olive oil
3 cloves garlic, sliced
2 medium white onions, cut lengthwise into thin rings
1½ lb fresh tomatoes, peeled, seeded, finely chopped
½ cup tomato juice
¼ cup fresh lime juice
¼ cup sliced, stuffed green olives
1 or 2 pickled jalapeño chilies, seeded, finely chopped
1 tbsp capers, drained
1 bay leaf
3 lb small red potatoes, cooked, skinned, cut in half
  chopped fresh coriander

Sprinkle fish with salt and pepper. Coat with flour and shake off excess. Heat oil in 12-inch skillet over medium heat. When hot, add garlic, stirring frequently until golden, 2 to 3 minutes. Remove garlic with slotted spoon and discard. Add as many fillets to skillet as will fit in a single layer without crowding. Cook over medium heat, turning once, until light brown, 2 minutes per side. Remove to plate. Repeat with remaining fillets. Add onions to skillet and sauté until soft. Stir in tomatoes, juices, olives, chilies, capers and bay leaf. Bring to a boil over high heat; reduce heat to low and simmer, covered for 15 minutes. Add any juices which have collected on the plate from the fish. Cook sauce over medium-high heat, stirring frequently, until thickened 2 to 3 minutes. Remove and discard bay leaf. Add fish to skillet, spoon sauce over fish and reduce heat to low. Simmer, covered, just until fish are opaque throughout, 3 to 5 minutes. Serve immediately with potatoes, garnished with coriander.
Serves 6.

Mousse de Kahlua

1 cup whipping cream
½ cup instant coffee powder
¼ cup Kahlua
2 tbsp sugar
1 egg white
2 tsp sugar
chocolate sprinkles

Chill bowl and beater before whipping cream. Combine cream and coffee powder in medium bowl. Beat until stiff. Add Kahlua and 2 tbsp sugar. Continue beating until very stiff. In a small bowl, beat egg white to soft peaks. Add 2 tsp sugar and beat until stiff. Fold into whipped cream mixture. Cover and chill. To serve, mound in dessert glasses and decorate with chocolate sprinkles.
Serves 6.

Aztec Fire

coffee
red wine
tequila
sugar
cocoa

Mix 1 cup hot, strong coffee with 2 oz red wine. Heat and pour into a glass. Add tequila and sugar to taste. Sprinkle with a dash of cocoa.

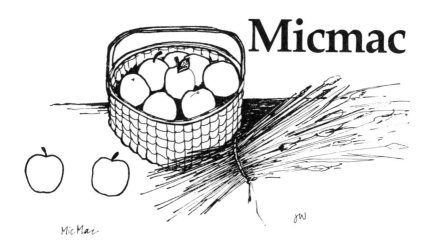

Mic Mac

Mustard Soup

1 lb fresh young mustard leaves
6 tbsp butter
6 tbsp flour
6 cups chicken stock
3 egg yolks
1 cup cream (heavy is best)
1 tsp salt
½ tsp white pepper

Clean and wash freshly picked mustard leaves under cold water. Drain well. In a 3- to 4-quart saucepan, melt 4 tbsp butter over high heat. When melted, lower heat and cook for 5 minutes, stirring constantly until roux is creamy and smooth. Remove from heat and add chicken broth, stirring with a whisk. Return to heat until thick and smooth. Add the mustard leaves, keeping a few for garnish. Cook over low heat for 25 minutes. Purée the soup in blender. Return to saucepan. Blend the egg yolks and cream (milk can also be used) and gradually add to the soup. Bring to a boil and simmer for 2 to 3 minutes. Taste and season with salt and pepper. Add reserved, shredded mustard leaves and the remaining 2 tbsp of butter. Serve in individual bowls.

Note: You may also use coltsfoot leaves, fiddleheads, dandelion or plantain.

Herb Dip

1 cup mayonnaise
1 tbsp lemon juice
2 large sprigs parsley, chopped
2 sprigs dill, chopped, or 1 tbsp dill seed put through blender
3 coltsfoot leaves, chopped
½ cup sour cream
½ tsp Worcestershire sauce
3 sprigs sweet marjoram, chopped
1 tbsp chopped chives
garlic powder

Combine all ingredients. Chill overnight so that all the flavours blend. Use as a dip for sticks of carrot or celery, cauliflower florets, broccoli or strips of green or red pepper.

Boiled Dressing for Dandelion Greens

1 egg, slightly beaten
dash pepper
1 tbsp flour
¼ cup cider
1 tsp salt
3 tbsp sugar
¾ cup milk

Mix all ingredients together in a pan over low heat. Don't worry about the lumps. Set aside to cool. It should be warm before pouring over dandelion greens.

Dandelion leaves may be used in soups, salads or sauces.

Burdock leaves may be eaten raw. The young leaf stalk may be used in a salad. They can also be peeled, cut in pieces and marinated in vinegar.

Evening primrose leaves, peeled of their skin, may be eaten raw or cooked as a vegetable. The root provides more variety.

Lamb's quarters, mint, purslane, dock, are all good in salads and soups, or sautéed with other vegetables.

Wood Sorrel and Sour Cream Dressing

2 cups wood sorrel leaves, finely chopped
1 cup water
1 cup sour cream
2 tsp sugar
1 tsp salt
½ tsp pepper

Clean and wash the leaves under cold running water. Boil water in a saucepan. Add the wood sorrel leaves and cook for 5 minutes. Remove from heat and let steep for 2 hours. Pour the sour cream into a large mixing bowl. Stir in sugar, salt, pepper and 4 tbsp of the cool wood sorrel juice. Beat with electric beater until dressing is smooth. Taste for seasoning. More wood sorrel juice may be added.

Cattail Greens

6 cattail shoots
2 tbsp butter
2 large onions, sliced
2 stalks celery, chopped
small piece green pepper, chopped

Gather cattails (when a foot high). Peel off outer leaves and chop the remainder. Heat frying pan and add butter. Add the cattails, onions, celery and green pepper. Sauté until all are tender. Cover and let sit for a few minutes. May be served as a vegetable side dish.

Baked Pumpkin

1 small pumpkin
2 tbsp apple cider
2 tbsp honey
2 tbsp butter or margarine, melted

Wash pumpkin well, place on pie pan and bake at 350°F for 1½ hours. Remove from oven and cut hole in top 3 to 4 inches in diameter; scoop out pulp and seeds. Mix together remaining ingredients; baste mixture over flesh of pumpkin, replace top, return to moderate oven and continue to bake 35 to 40 minutes, basting occasionally. Serve whole, scooping out portions at the table or cut into wedges as you would a melon. Ladle a little of the cider mixture over each serving.

Plantain Casserole

1 lb plantain leaves
2 tbsp butter
3 onions, finely chopped
1 lb ground beef
1 can tomato soup
potato chips

Clean and rinse the plantain leaves under cold running water. In a skillet over high heat melt the butter. Add onions and brown slightly. Lower heat and add ground beef. Brown. Line a greased casserole with plantain leaves. Add a layer of the beef mixture, then a layer of plantain leaves. Continue until all is used, finishing with a layer of the plantain leaves. Pour tomato soup over the greens and sprinkle with crushed potato chips. Bake at 350°F for 2 hours.

Cold Chicken and Wild Vegetable Salad

3 or 4 whole chicken breasts
salt and pepper to taste
4 coltsfoot leaves
1 cup fiddlehead greens
dash Worcestershire sauce
2 tbsp red wine vinegar
½ tsp marjoram
½ cup sour cream
1 can pineapple chunks, drained
1 head of lettuce
bunch of seedless grapes

Simmer chicken breasts, seasoned to your taste for 1½ hours. Remove meat; drain, cool and cube. Finely chop the coltsfoot leaves. Cook fiddleheads in salted water, drain well and chop. Add seasonings to sour cream and combine with chicken, coltsfoot and fiddleheads. Chop pineapple and add. Serve on lettuce leaves with grape garnish.

Shortbread mould.

Scotland

Cock-a-Leekie Soup

1 boiling fowl
2 to 3 large onions
leaves and outer stalks from head of celery
2 qts salted water
½ cup barley
4 leeks
salt and pepper
parsley

On the day before required, bring fowl (including giblets and neck), onions, celery and salted water to a boil. Simmer 2½ hours. Remove fowl, strain stock, discard vegetables and refrigerate stock overnight. The next day, skim off fat and return to a boil. Soak barley in 1 cup water for a few minutes, drain, rinse and add to stock. Wash leeks thoroughly, cut in small pieces and add to stock with salt and pepper. Simmer 30 minutes or until barley is soft. Snip parsley with kitchen shears and add just before serving. If desired, a little of the meat may be added but this is not necessary as the broth has enough body on its own. It is more practical to use the cooked meat in salads, sandwiches, etc.

Scotch Broth

1 cup dried green peas
½ cup navy beans
1 meaty soup bone
4 quarts water
1 cup pearl barley
3 medium potatoes, diced
3 large onions, chopped
3 medium carrots, diced
1 cup diced turnip
1 cup diced celery

Soak peas and beans in water overnight. Simmer soup bone 3 hours, in 4 quarts water. Add barley, peas and beans and cook another hour. Add vegetables and continue to cook for 1 hour. Season to taste with salt and pepper.

Rob Roy's Oat Bread

3 cups boiling water
2 cups rolled oats
¼ cup shortening
2 tsp sugar
1 cup lukewarm water
2 envelopes yeast
⅔ cup table molasses
4 tsp salt
8 to 8½ cups flour

Pour boiling water over oats and shortening. Stir until shortening melts and let stand 20 minutes. Dissolve 2 tsp sugar in lukewarm water. Over this, sprinkle yeast. Let stand 10 minutes and stir briskly. Stir molasses and salt into oat mixture. Add softened yeast and stir. Beat in 2½ cups flour and mix thoroughly. Gradually beat in additional flour. Work in by hand if necessary. Turn out onto floured surface. Knead 8 to 10 minutes. Shape into a smooth ball and place in a greased bowl. Cover and let rise until doubled. Punch down and shape into four loaves. Place in greased loaf pans, grease tops, cover and let rise until doubled, about 1 hour. Bake at 400°F for 30 to 35 minutes.

Oat Cakes

1 tsp baking soda
¾ cup cold water
2½ cups fine oatmeal
1 cup flour
1 tsp salt
1 heaping tbsp sugar
½ cup lard

Dissolve soda in water. Mix oatmeal, flour, salt, sugar and lard, rubbing them together with your hands. Roll out thin and cut into squares. Bake at 400°F for approximately 8 minutes.

Clapshot

1 lb potatoes
1 lb turnips
1 tbsp freshly cut chives
lump of butter or drippings
salt and pepper

Boil potatoes and turnips and mash them together. Add chives, butter, salt and pepper. Mix thoroughly and serve very hot. May be used to accompany haggis.

Skirlie

2 oz suet*
2 onions, chopped
¼ lb medium oatmeal (approximately)
salt and pepper

Chop suet and place in a hot frying pan. When melted, stir in onions and fry until brown. Stir in oatmeal until mixture is fairly thick. Season to taste with salt and pepper. Serve hot with mashed potatoes or bacon.

Note: Suet from the butcher is preferred to shredded suet for this recipe.

Bashed Neeps

1 large turnip (cut after frost)
1 level tsp salt
1 oz butter
pepper
pinch grated nutmeg
1 tbsp cream

Peel turnip and cut into large pieces. Place in saucepan and cover with cold water. Add salt. Simmer until tender. Mash until smooth and blend with butter, nutmeg and pepper. Add cream and serve.

Canadian Haggis

1 lb lean ground beef
1 lb lean ground lamb
1 medium onion, chopped finely
¾ cup oatmeal
pinch salt
pinch ground ginger
pinch garlic
pinch cayenne
pinch oregano
pinch basil
pinch thyme
¾ cup beef bouillon cube stock
1 tbsp finely ground suet
¼ tsp black pepper

Stir-fry beef and lamb until brown. Mix all ingredients carefully and place in coffee can(s). Steam 2½ to 3 hours. Unmould and cut in thin slices. May be used as a pâté or served with clapshot.

Scots Diet Loaf

2 cups (1 lb) butter
2 cups fine granulated sugar
10 eggs, separated
3½ cups flour
½ tsp mace
½ tsp grated lemon rind

Cream butter. Add sugar gradually, beating until fluffy. Beat egg yolks until very thick and light in colour. Add. Beat egg whites until stiff and fold in. Blend in flour, mace and lemon rind. Beat 5 minutes. Bake in greased and floured pans, or a tube pan, for about one hour at 300°F.
Note: This very old recipe, the ancestor of pound cake, was mentioned by Sir Walter Scott in his writings. Copied from *The Highlanders Cook Book.*

Inverness Gingerbread

1 cup rolled oats
1 cup butter
1½ cups dark molasses
3 cups sifted flour
½ cup candied lemon peel (minced)
4 tbsp grated fresh green ginger or 2 tbsp ground ginger
¼ cup cream

Measure oats, then grind them or run briefly in blender. Cream butter until light and fluffy and blend in molasses. Mix in flour, oats, peel and ginger. Last, stir in the cream. Bake in a greased and floured 9- x 14-inch pan at 350°F for 45 minutes. Cut in squares to serve.
Note: This recipe, with no eggs or baking powder, sounds as if it can't possibly work. But it does and it's delicious! It makes an old-fashioned, rich, dark gingerbread. Copied from *The Highlanders Cook Book.*

Rob Roy's Maids of Honour

pastry
raspberry jam
½ cup butter
1 cup white sugar
2 eggs, beaten
2 cups flour
4 tsp baking powder
1 cup milk
1 tsp almond flavouring

Line small muffin or tart tins with pastry. Cover with raspberry jam. Make a batter from remaining ingredients and pour over jam, making sure that batter sticks to sides of pastry. Bake at 350°F until golden brown. Top with icing made from icing sugar and water.
Makes 40.

Rob Roy's Shortbread

1 lb (2 to 3½ cups) flour
pinch salt
½ cup sugar
1½ cups butter

Sift dry ingredients and rub in butter until crumbly. Knead until smooth and holding together. Divide dough in half. Shape into rounds about ½ inch thick. Cut into wedges. Prick lightly with a fork. Bake at 325°F for 20 to 30 minutes. DO NOT OVERBAKE. Remove from oven and sprinkle with sugar while still hot. Store in airtight container.

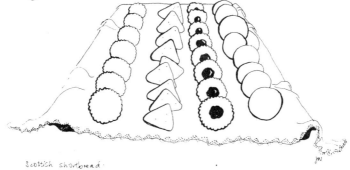

Scottish shortbread·

Rich Cream Scones

2 cups sifted flour
1 tbsp baking powder
2 tbsp sugar
½ tsp salt
⅓ cup butter
1 egg
½ cup cream
¼ cup currants
1 egg white

Mix flour, baking powder, sugar and salt. Cut in butter. Mix in egg and cream. Stir in currants. Turn onto floured board and pat into a round, ½ inch thick. Cut into wedges. Brush tops with egg white and sprinkle with sugar. Bake at 400°F for 15 to 18 minutes.

Rock Buns

1½ cups self-rising flour
1 tsp salt
⅓ cup butter or margarine
⅓ cup sugar
⅓ cup sultanas
finely grated lemon peel
1 egg
4 tbsp milk

Sift flour and salt. Cut in butter and rub into flour. Stir in sugar. Add sultanas and peel. Beat egg and milk together and add to mixture. Mixture should be coarse. Place twelve heaping spoonfuls a little apart on greased tray. Bake at 400°F for 20 to 25 minutes.

Mustard Pickles

3 quarts chopped, peeled cucumber
1 quart chopped onions
1 medium cauliflower, cut small
2 sweet red peppers, chopped
½ cup pickling salt
2 cups chopped celery

Sauce
1½ quarts vinegar (reserve 1½ to 2 cups to make a paste)
6 cups white sugar
¼ cup mustard
½ oz turmeric
½ oz celery seed
2 oz mustard seed

Place cucumbers, onions, cauliflower and peppers in a large bowl. Add salt and cover with cold water. Let stand overnight and drain well in the morning. Add celery.

Sauce: Bring vinegar to a boil. Make a paste with reserved vinegar and other ingredients. Add paste to boiling vinegar. Add vegetables. Return to a boil and cook for 5 minutes. Bottle in sterilized jars.

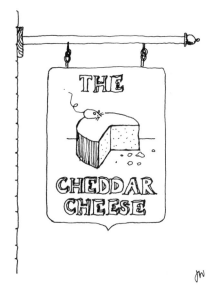

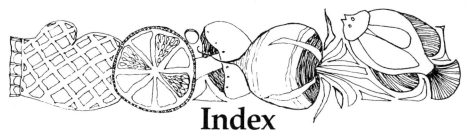

Index